ABOUT THE AUTHOR

Eric Leuenberger, known as "The Ecommerce Expert," is a Google certified professional and founder of Voom Ventures, LLC, a consulting firm whose products and services help online retailers achieve higher conversion rates, maximize ROI, decrease expenses, and increase revenue.

Eric's over two decades of proven experience, coupled with his passion to help ecommerce stores achieve sustainable growth and increase profits, has gained him the reputation as a knowledgeable, trustworthy resource and the "go to guy" for those seeking to generate more sales online.

His portfolio of successes includes working with enterprise level corporations including The British Broadcasting Corporation, eBay, and P&G to help them increase productivity of their online initiatives. In addition to working with enterprise corporations, he has also assisted small to mid-sized ecommerce organizations and start-ups across seven different countries reach their online objectives.

To find out more, visit www.TheEcommerceExpert.com

Google Analytics Uncovered

How to Set Up and Maximize Ecommerce Data in Google Analytics

ERIC LEUENBERGER

Google Analytics Uncovered: How to Set Up and Maximize Ecommerce Data in Google Analytics

Copyright © 2018 Voom Ventures, LLC.

To my parents. For without them I would not be who I am today.

CONTENTS

INTRODUCTION

This guide was developed based on a six-part article series I wrote on Google Analytics. In that series, called Google Analytics Demystified, I talked about the various components that make up Google Analytics, went over some installation issues, and explained the difference between each of them.

In this guide, I'll recap some of that information so you have everything in one convenient location. In addition, this guide contains a number of screenshots to better illustrate the steps needed to set up and utilize the various components within Google Analytics so that you can get the most out of your data and use that information to increase your website conversion.

What This Guide Is

This guide is an instructional manual and aid. Its purpose is to give you a sounding board upon which you can confidently implement and interpret what Google Analytics is telling you.

This guide is not all inclusive, and should be used as a supplemental tool to aid you in working with Google Analytics. Reading analytic data is one thing: Properly interpreting and understanding what it means for your business is another thing altogether. With time comes knowledge and with practice comes success. There is no substitute for a good set of "human eyes" and a thorough understanding of website analytics in general.

What This Guide Is Not

This guide and any supplementary tools referenced are not intended to be an overnight crash course that turns you into an analytics guru. After reading this book, you will understand some of the basic reporting features available within Google Analytics as well as begin to understand how to use that data to make objective business decisions. Fully comprehending the data takes repeated practice, a careful eye, and time; none of which can be provided in this guide.

This guide is not intended to answer all of your questions: It is a stepping stone on your path to successfully understanding how Google Analytics is set up, what types of information it can provide you with, and how to link together some critical components that provide you with more information on your business.

Who Can Benefit From Using This Guide

- Anyone currently using or thinking of using Google Analytics as a tracking system for a website.

- Anyone already using Google Analytics who wants to gain more insight into its various components and learn how to use them to gather better reporting information about a website.

- Anyone that wants a better understanding of how Google Analytics works.

How This Guide Is Set Up

This guide starts with an introduction to what Google Analytics is and explains how it can help you achieve better results from your website. You will learn how to create a Google account, sign up for a Google Analytics account, create website profiles, add multiple users through the Access Manager, and create filters to exclude certain visitors from your statistics.

In the first few sections, I also briefly touch upon the meaning of "conversion rate" as well as go into a few examples of how to calculate it. I provide a few illustrations to show you the importance of conversion rates, and what they can mean to your business if monitored carefully.

The remaining sections of the guide break down each of the four components that make up Google Analytics and explain how you can utilize them to increase the conversion of your website to make better business decisions.

Finally, I close by allowing you to quiz yourself on the knowledge you have learned through studying the guide and put your knowledge to the test by presenting a number of exercises that use hands-on techniques.

How to Use This Guide

There is no right or wrong way to use this guide. Some readers may be familiar with a number of the concepts presented and may elect to skip ahead to sections that they need to brush up on.

Others may find it helpful to start from the beginning and read it cover to cover.

The choice is yours. And all routes will lead to a happy ending.

What This Guide Will Teach You

This guide will teach you how to set up, implement, and utilize the four main components of Google Analytics including "Vanilla" Google Analytics, ecommerce tracking, conversion tracking, and sales goals and funnels.

More important, it will teach you how to use your analytics data as a tool to increase conversion by reading, understanding, and interpreting it. I'll show you a few important statistics you should be aware of in your reports that, when addressed, can help you set a proper plan of action for increasing conversion.

1

GOOGLE ANALYTICS

What Is Google Analytics?

Wikipedia defines Google Analytics as follows:

"Google Analytics (GA) is a free service offered by Google that generates detailed statistics about the visitors to a website. Its main highlight is that a webmaster can optimize their Google Ads advertisement and marketing campaigns through the use of GA's analysis of where the visitors came from, how long they stayed on the website and their geographical position.

Most important, a webmaster can define and track conversions, or goals. Goals might include sales, lead generation, viewing a specific page, or downloading a particular file. By using this tool, marketers can determine which ads are performing, and which are not, as well as find unexpected sources of quality visitors."

Why You Need Google Analytics and How It Can Help You

If you want to learn more about how effectively your website is currently performing, or how you can gather additional data to help it perform even better; if you want to more effectively target your website visitors and increase your conversion, you should consider Google Analytics.

If you want to increase the effectiveness of your Google Ads campaigns and determine precisely which keywords convert and which do not, you should consider Google Analytics.

It's a powerful free tool that performs nicely for most businesses and it will give you the data necessary to make more effective business decisions about how to better target your visitors.

"You cannot manage what you do not measure." – Peter Drucker

It's difficult to spot individual problem areas and manage for incremental improvements if you don't measure to see what is getting better and what isn't.

What You Can Learn From Using Google Analytics

Google Analytics "talks" to you. If you listen, you'll discover a wealth of information that will assist you in increasing your website conversion.

On a general level, Google Analytics reports to you how people find your site and what they do when they get there.

On a business level, the data gathered through Google Analytics can help you improve your website user experience, help you increase your return on investment, and even increase sales. When analytics is set up correctly, you'll gain access to a number of key performance indicators (KPIs) including, but not limited to, conversion rate.

What Is Conversion Rate, How Is It Calculated, and What Can It Mean for Your Business?

The measure that identifies how efficiently your website turns visitors into prospects and/or customers is called the conversion rate.

Conversion rate is calculated by dividing the total completed website actions like product sales, email opt-ins, or registrations by the total number of unique visitors to the website within a specific period of time.

The calculation for conversion rate is:

Total Completed Website Actions / Total Unique Visitors

For example, if 5,000 unique visitors arrive at your website and 50 of them purchased your product, then your conversion rate is 1 percent calculated as follows:

50 product purchases / 5,000 unique visitors = 1 percent conversion rate

So, what can an increase in conversion mean to your business? Well, let me briefly illustrate using the following side-by-side comparison and the above starting figures as an example:

Sales Results at 1 Percent Conversion	Sales Results at 3 Percent Conversion
Est. Unique Visitors: 5,000	Est. Unique Visitors: 5,000
Conversion Rate: 1 percent	Conversion Rate: 3 percent
Average Sales Price: $75	Average Sales Price: $75
Total Revenue: $3,750	Total Revenue: $11,250
	$7,500 Increase!

Now you should have a very top-level understanding of what Google Analytics is, why you need it, how it can help you increase conversion, and how you can personally calculate your conversion rate.

Conveniently, Google Analytics automatically calculates your conversion rate for you if you have the right tracking components in place. (I'll show you how to install them and set them up later in this guide.) Still, it is nice to know how to arrive at the figure yourself; if for no other reason than to determine where your conversion currently stands so you can measure it against what Google reports once you have the components installed.

Organizational Structure of Google Analytics

The illustration below shows a sample organizational structure for two Analytics accounts. This will help you better understand the foundational components introduced in the next several sections as you set up your Analytics account.

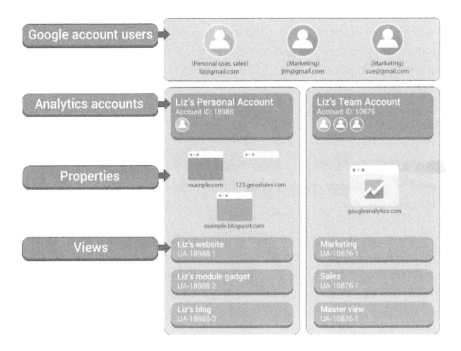

Image Source: Google

As shown above, the hierarchy of a Google Analytics account is as follows: Users have access to a specific Analytics account either by creating it themselves or by being given access from someone else. The Analytics account could contain one or multiple properties, each with its own tracking ID that represents a unique site, mobile app, or device. To organize and segment data even further, each property has one or more views. A view can be used to segment and filter data for producing differing reports.

You can grant additional users permission to view the data at any of the three levels. I'll talk more about how to do this later.

Analytics Properties

An Analytics property is a website, mobile app, or device (e.g. a kiosk or point-of-sale device.) An account can contain one or more properties and each property has its own unique tracking ID. The ID links the property to one or more views.

Example: In a property that has the tracking code UA-12345-1, 12345 is the account number and 1 represents the view. A second view for the same account would have a number 2 in the place of the 1 (e.g. UA-12345-2) and so on for each additional view created.

Analytics Views

A view is the lowest level of the Analytics account and it represents the actual reported data that appears from a given property (e.g. graphs, metrics, etc.).

Sometimes it can be useful to have multiple views for a single property with each view made up of various filters to include or exclude certain data. Examples might be creating a filtered view that removes internal traffic (traffic from your own company) from the reports, or creating a view that replaces query string parameters at the end of a URL with simplified more user readable URLs.

Getting Started With Google Analytics

Google Analytics is a Google product and as such, you need a Google account to use it. If you do not already have a Google account, create one by going to google.com.

Follow the on-screen prompts to create your account.

If you already have a Google account that includes other Google products you use (such as Google Ads, Google My Business, Search Console,

Google Drive, etc.) it is recommended that you use that same account to create an Analytics account. This makes it easier to tie everything together later by linking each product.

If you already have an Analytics account, you can skip to step 4.

Please note that some of the screenshots you see are taken from websites that change over time. Although these screenshots might be slightly different from what you see currently, the process of creating your account remains basically the same.

Step 1. Create a Google Account

Create a Google account by providing the requested information.

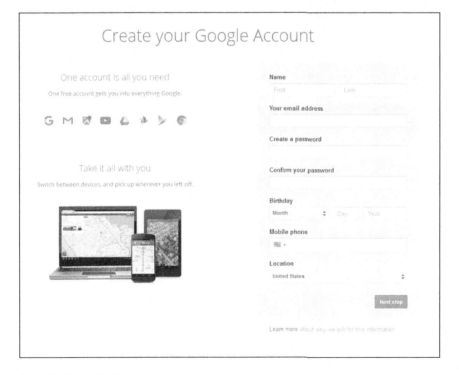

Step 2. Sign Up for Analytics

After you create your Google account, you may now sign up for a Google Analytics account by going to google.com/analytics/

Click the **Sign Up** button to continue the setup of the Analytics portion of your account.

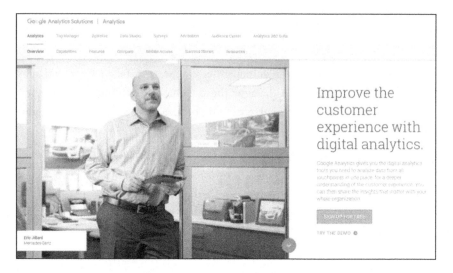

Step 3. Create an Analytics Account

The first step in creating a Google Analytics account is to give the account a name. You can name it anything you want, but I recommend using the name of the company associated with the properties that will be tracked, such as ABC Company.

During the initial setup, Google also has you create your first property. The property is where the actual tracking code comes from. I recommend naming this something that represents the domains and/or subdomains that will be contained here for tracking. Using the ABC Company as an example, in this case the property might be named "abccompany.com" because it could contain "shop.abccompany.com" and "www.abccompany.com" yet both represent the overall main domain.

Next you will be prompted to choose an industry. This is not required and will not affect your data in any way. It simply helps Google make future improvements based on industry data it gathers.

Finally, select a reporting time zone and agree to the terms if asked.

Create additional properties as needed. Property creation is covered later in this chapter.

Step 4. Get the Tracking Code

Once you have set up your account you will receive the tracking code to enter into your site.

If you don't see the tracking code, click the **Admin** link near the bottom left side of the navigation pane.

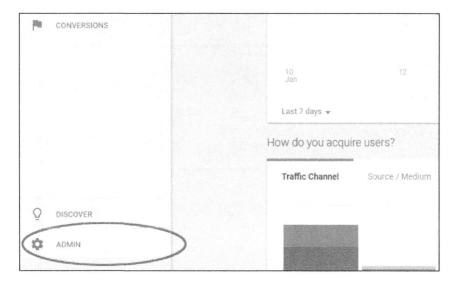

Then follow the numbers below to find your tracking code.

Copy and paste the code onto every page that you want to track on your site. If your site utilizes dynamic footers, simply placing it into one file will more than likely place it on every page of your website. If your web framework utilizes plugins to automatically add the tracking code to the site, follow the instructions provided with that plugin to insert the code.

If you are uncertain about where to place the code, ask your technical support team.

Congratulations! You have now successfully completed the setup of your Google account, and signed up for a Google Analytics account as well. Now it's time to get on with the various tracking components available to you within Google Analytics.

Creating Website Properties

Google Analytics allows you to track multiple websites or mobile apps from one convenient location so that you do not have to create multiple Google Analytics accounts. You can do that by adding what are called website properties to your main account. Each property will be assigned a unique tracking ID and code (that must be inserted using the same steps listed in the above section).

Keep in mind that data metrics for resources tagged with the same ID are collected into the corresponding property.

In other words, if a single property ID is associated with two websites, data for both of those sites will appear in the same property in your Analytics account. If you choose this route, you can use views and filters to organize the data. In addition, you can further segregate that data using segments from the report level.

Before you create a new website property, consider your business objectives. In certain circumstances you might want two different websites sending data to the same property. In other cases, you may want to make sure the two websites each have their own set of data independent of the other.

To add a new website property to your account, do the following:

1. Log in to your Google Analytics account.

2. From the left navigation pane, click on the gear icon.

3. Select the drop-down option under the property section and click on **Create new property**. To add a new property, choose website or mobile app depending on what you are tracking, and follow the instructions on the page.

New Property

Creating a new property will provide you with a Tracking ID.

When your initial property is created, we will also create a default view that will gather all data associated probably want to create a second reporting view, and you will need to create and apply one or more view

What would you like to track?

Website   Mobile app

Tracking Method

This property works using Universal Analytics. Click *Get Tracking ID* and implement the Universal Analyti

Setting up your property

Website Name

My New Website

Website URL

http:// ▾   Example: http://www.mywebsite.com

Industry Category ?

Select One ▾

Reporting Time Zone

United States ▾   (GMT-08:00) Pacific Time ▾

This account has 4 properties. The maximum is 50.

Get Tracking ID   Cancel

Congratulations! You have just completed adding a new website property to your existing Google Analytics account.

Creating Reporting Views

A reporting view is created the same way a website property is.

1. Log in to your Google Analytics account.

2. From the left navigation pane, click on the gear icon.

3. Select the drop-down option under the view section and click on **Create new view**. Choose website or mobile app depending on what you are tracking, and follow the instructions on the page.

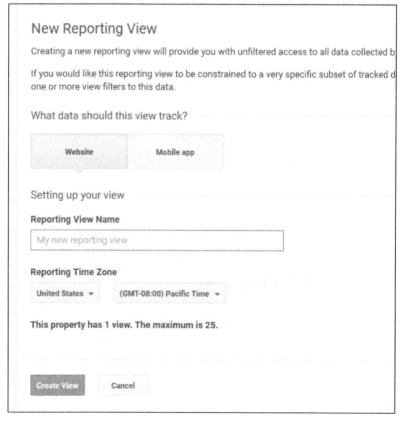

Congratulations! You have just completed adding a new reporting view to your existing Google Analytics property.

Giving Access to Outside Users

There may be times when you want to allow others to view your Analytics. Rather than give them your login information, you should grant them access through the user management feature. What access level you give them depends on your individual needs and the role the individual plays in your business.

You can grant access at the account level, property level, and the view level. Be aware of what level you are granting access, and to whom you are granting it. Granting access at the account level gives access to everything under it, as well as all properties and views.

To give a user access to your Analytics, do the following:

1. Log in to your Google Analytics account.

2. Click **Admin (also shown as a gear icon).**

3. Click **User Management** in the **Account, Property,** or **View** column.

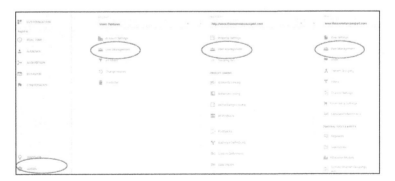

4. Click the **+** sign (usually in the upper right corner of the screen) to add a new user.

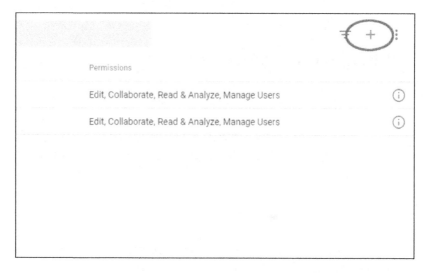

5. Complete the form, select the access permissions, and add the new user. If you want the new user to only be able to read reports, then select the **Read & Analyze** option.

Creating View Filters

Filters can be useful for a number of reasons including to report only on a subdomain or directory, to exclude traffic from a specific domain or IP address, or to take dynamic page URLs and convert them into readable text strings.

Filters can be created at the account level and then applied to multiple views or created at the individual view level. Common filters that are the same from view to view are easier to manage when created at the account level and then applied to multiple views.

Note that filters are applied to the data in the order that they were created. So if the view already has a filter, any new filters created will be applied after that. You can adjust the order of these filters at the view level.

Be aware that filters are permanent, irreversible, and destructive to data. Although this sounds like a reason to never use filters, that's not the case. Filters can be very helpful. However, because filters are applied after the data has been processed, once you apply one, it permanently includes, or excludes data for the view you are tracking. To make sure you don't lose any data within your view, always keep an unfiltered view of your data in addition to creating a new filtered view. Never apply a filter to the *only* data view you have.

At the time of this writing, Google Analytics provides several predefined filter types and a number of custom options as well.

Predefined filter options:

- **Include or Exclude traffic from the domains:** Use this filter to include or exclude traffic from a specific domain, such as an ISP or company network.

- **Include or Exclude traffic from the IP addresses:** This filter works to include or exclude clicks from certain sources. You can enter a single IP address, or a range of addresses.

- **Include or Exclude traffic to the subdirectories:** Use this filter if you want a profile to report only on a particular subdirectory (such as www.example.com/soccer).

- **Include or Exclude traffic to the hostname:** This filter is handy if you find that your Analytics is reporting data from *another* domain outside of yours. That's right, someone could take your analytics code and drop it onto their site. This "Analytics spam" results in inflated statistics that don't even belong to your domain.

Using an exclude hostname filter would be one way to remedy this problem and get rid of the outside influence.

Custom filter options:

- **Exclude Pattern:** This type of filter excludes log file lines (hits) that match the filter pattern. Matching lines are ignored in their entirety; for example, a filter that excludes Netscape will also exclude all other information in that log line, such as visitor, path, referral, and domain information.

- **Include Pattern:** This type of filter includes log file lines (hits) that match the filter pattern. All non-matching hits will be ignored and any data in non-matching hits is unavailable to the reports.

- **Search & Replace:** This simple filter can be used to search for a pattern within a field and replace the found pattern with an alternate form.

- **Advanced:** This type of filter allows you to build a field from one or two other fields. The filtering engine will apply the expressions in the two Extract fields to the specified fields and then construct a field using the Constructor expression.

- **Uppercase/Lowercase:** Converts the contents of the field into all uppercase or all lowercase characters. These filters only affect letters, and will not affect characters or numbers.

Common uses for filters:

- **Exclude internal traffic from your reports:** You can set up a filter to exclude all internal IP addresses (example would be traffic from your company intranet) you don't want included in reports.

- **Report on activity in specific directories:** To track activity for only a specific directory on your site, set up an Include filter and indicate only that directory in the parameters. Want to track all activity for the site except a particular directory? Follow the same steps, but change it to an exclude filter.

- **Track subdomains in separate views:** If you want separate reporting for multiple subdomains (example would be www.yoursite.com, yoursite.com, and members.yoursite.com), then create a view for each subdomain and use an include filter to identify only activity to each specific subdirectory.

Important notes when using filters:

- Never apply a filter to the *only* data view you have; doing so could cause you to permanently lose data within that view.

- Filters can take up to 24 hours before they are applied to your data.

- In addition, filters are account level objects. This means that if you change a filter at the view level, it will change it for *all* views which share that filter. If you would like to customize a filter for an individual view, create the filter at the individual view level itself (rather than at the account level).

Excluding Certain Traffic From Statistical Tracking

You can exclude certain users or traffic from tracking by setting up filters within your Google Analytics property. You may want to do this if, for example, you do not want your own activity to be recorded in the statistics.

This can be important because if you frequent your website, whether for performing work, adding content, or just looking around, each move you make will be recorded in the statistics for that site. As a result, the data gathered may be skewed and so will the factors you are using to measure the efficiency of your website.

For this reason, you may want to exclude yourself and any other users whose activity on the site should not count toward your final measurements.

You have a few options for excluding internal traffic from your reports. If you aren't familiar with coding, some of the steps required for creating these exclusions may seem intimidating. I've included explicit instructions, but if you feel overwhelmed, seek help from an IT professional.

You can exclude it by IP address (or range of IP addresses), by domain, or by using cookies. If you have a dynamic IP address (one that changes and does not stay the same), then you may want to use the cookie option to exclude yourself from reports.

Instructions on how to implement each of the options are below:

Excluding traffic by IP address

With filters, you can exclude a single IP address or a range of IP addresses. You have two options for doing this. You can create either a custom filter or use a predefined filter. Both methods are described in the steps below.

In some cases (especially when setting up custom IP filters) you'll want to use what are called regular expressions to set up your filter. Regular expressions provide a concise and flexible means for matching strings of text, such as particular characters, words, or patterns of characters. They can be simple or complex to work with and understand.

For a little help, go to google.com and search "google analytics regular expression builder."

To set up an exclude filter for a single IP address, follow these steps:

1. From the **View** column on the administration page, choose the view you want to add the filter to from the drop-down and click **Filters.**

2. Enter a **Filter Name** for this filter and choose the predefined **Filter Type.** (The filter type you choose here will determine if it would be best to use regular expressions or not.) Name the filter something that it represents so it's easy to identify in reporting. For example: Exclude internal traffic from office.

3. If you chose **Predefined,** from the drop-down list, select **Exclude traffic from the IP addresses.**

4. Enter the correct value of the IP address you wish to exclude in the space provided.

5. Click **Save** to save this filter, or **Cancel** to return to the previous page.

If you have multiple IP addresses you would like to exclude, rather than create a new filter for each IP address, you can use a regular expression to exclude them all with one filter. To set up an exclude filter for a range of IP addresses follow these steps:

1. From the **View** column on the administration page, choose the view you want to add the filter to from the drop-down and click **Filters.**

2. Enter a **Filter Name** for this filter.

3. Under **Filter Type,** choose **Custom.**

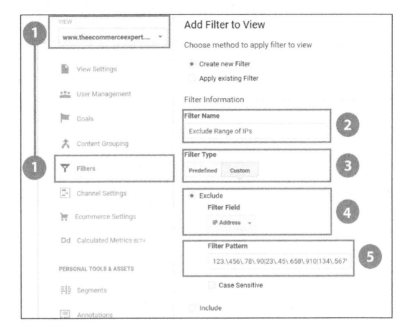

4. Choose the **Exclude** filter and select **IP Address** from the drop-down field.

5. Enter your **Filter Pattern** for each of the IP addresses you wish to exclude using the following example format:

    123\.456\.78\.90 | 23\.45\.658\.910 | 134\.567\.890\.234

    Escape all periods with a forward slash and separate unique IP addresses with the | delimiter. You may also create more complex regular expressions to eliminate a full range (hundreds) of IP addresses with very little code.

    If you are not familiar with how to create regular expressions, you can find more information on the internet.

6. Click **Save** to finalize your changes.

Dynamic IP address considerations

If you have a dynamic IP address (one that doesn't remain the same) then you won't likely be able to use the IP filtering method described above. Instead you'll need to set a cookie so that when you visit your site from the computer with the cookie, you will not be tracked.

How do you know if you have a dynamic IP Address? If you use your computer in various locations (i.e. from a laptop that you move from place to place) or if you connect to the internet through a provider out of your home, chances are you are using a dynamic IP address.

Excluding traffic by setting cookies

To exclude traffic from dynamic IP addresses, you can use a JavaScript function to set a cookie on each computer that you use to access the site. Once the cookie is set, you'll then be able to filter all visitors with this cookie from appearing on your Analytics reports.

There are a few options available for excluding dynamic IP addresses using cookies.

1. You can set your browser to not accept cookies for the particular domain you wish to be excluded from reporting on.

2. You can use tracking code on a page only you have access to that sets a cookie and creates a custom dimension. You then create a new filter at the view level to exclude this dimension.

If you are choose option 2 above, the following steps need to be completed:

- Set up the tracking code.

- Configure the custom dimension in Analytics.

- Create and apply the filter.

Each is explained in the next three sections.

Set up the tracking code

Create a single page on your site that only you will access. You don't want it accessed by search engines so make sure to put a **noindex, nofollow** on it as well, and don't link to it from other pages on the site.

Add the following tracking code to the page (replacing UA-XXXXX-Y with your Tracking ID and edit the dimension1 variable with whatever term you want to identify this traffic. I recommend something like **excludemyself**.

```
<!DOCTYPE HTML PUBLIC "-//W3C//DTD HTML 4.01
Transitional//EN">
<html>
<head>
    <title>Google Analytics Cookie Set</title>
    <meta name="robots" content="noindex, nofollow">

<!-- Google Analytics -->
<script>
(function(i,s,o,g,r,a,m){i['GoogleAnalyticsObject']=r;i[r]=
i[r]||function(){
(i[r].q=i[r].q||[]).push(arguments)},i[r].l=1*new
Date();a=s.createElement(o),
m=s.getElementsByTagName(o)[0];a.async=1;a.src=g;m.parentNo
de.insertBefore(a,m)
})(window,document,'script','//www.google-
analytics.com/analytics.js','ga');

ga('create', 'UA-XXXXX-Y', 'auto');
ga('send', 'pageview', {
  'dimension1': 'excludemyself'
});

</script>
<!-- End Google Analytics -->

</head>
<body>
<p>This page just set a cookie on your machine for
excluding your computer from your Google Analytics
reports.</p>

<p>To complete the process, you must now login to your
Google Analytics account and create a Custom Dimension and
Custom Filter if you haven't done so already.</p>
</body>
</html>
```

Once the page is created and the tracking code is in place, upload it to your server and then access it using your browser. (If you use multiple browsers, you will need to access it from every browser you use.) You will need to revisit the page whenever you clear your cookies.

Now the cookie is set and it's time to create the custom dimension.

Configure the custom dimension

1. Select the **Admin** tab and navigate to the property that you want to add the custom dimension to.

2. In the **Property** column, click **Custom Definitions**, then click **Custom Dimensions**.

3. Click **+ New Custom Dimension**.

4. Give the custom dimension a name. (You can name it anything you want. I recommend something like Exclude Myself From Traffic).

5. Select **Scope** (in this instance it needs to be **User**).

6. Check the **Active** checkbox.

7. Click **Create** and then click **Done**.

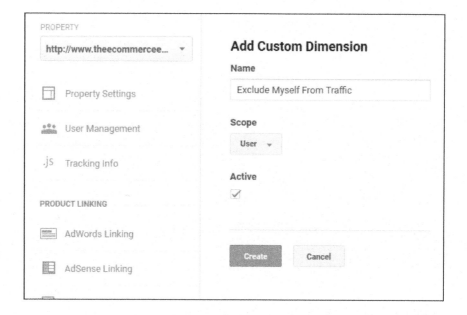

Configure the filter

The filter is used to exclude the traffic we identified using the custom dimension. Add the filter, taking care to apply the filter at the view level, not the account level.

The exclude filter should look like this:

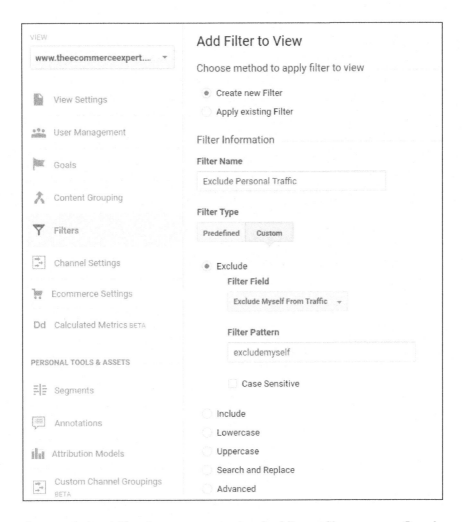

Congratulations! You have now completed adding a filter to your Google Analytics account that will exclude all traffic that contains the cookie you just set.

Setup Complete: Now What?

So far you have learned how to create a Google account, sign up for Google Analytics, create multiple properties, create views under each property, create filters to exclude certain traffic from your reports, and grant access to different users. You have also learned what conversion rate is, how to calculate it, and why it is important for your business.

Moving forward you'll learn about some of the main tracking components available through Google Analytics. These components determine the types of reporting data available in your Google Analytics account and enable you to improve your website in order to increase conversion.

2

"VANILLA" GOOGLE ANALYTICS

What Is "Vanilla" Google Analytics?

"Vanilla" Google Analytics is the name I give to the basic or standard tracking code you are given when you initially sign up for a Google Analytics account. (Think of it as the "out of the box" tracking code.) Installing it alone provides basic tracking capabilities, but it does not activate ecommerce tracking, conversion tracking, or goal tracking, the elements you need to measure progress toward your objectives.

On its own, the standard code is okay, but when combined with other components available inside Google Analytics, it becomes the foundation of a powerful tracking system.

"Vanilla" Google Analytics tracking is the nuts and bolts of the total tracking system. You must have "Vanilla" Google Analytics in place before you can add the other tracking components because they rely on the foundation that it provides.

How to Install "Vanilla" Google Analytics Tracking

There are several options for installing the tracking code on your site. With the popularity of Google Analytics, many content management systems (CMSs), such as WordPress, and applications provide complete integration via plugins. If your system has that option, then by all means use it.

If you don't have a plugin to use, there are two other options for installing the tracking code:

- Manual installation

- Google Tag Manager

Installation Option 1: Manual Installation

Now that you have a Google Analytics account, you need to install the tracking code onto your website.

To do that, log in to your Google Analytics account, click the **Admin** link, under the **Property** column. select the website you want the tracking code for, click **Tracking Info,** and then **Tracking Code**.

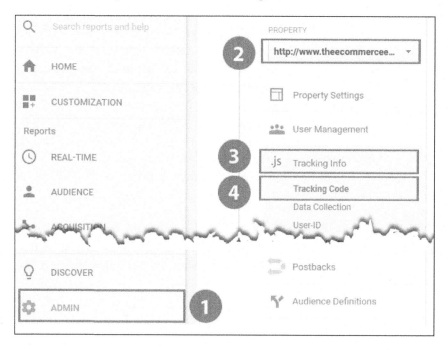

Your screen should now look like the following:

Copy and paste the tracking code from the page into your site following the instructions provided on the screen.

To check if your tracking code is installed and set up correctly, look at the **Status** section of the page. When you first install the code on your site (or when there are problems with the code), the status will indicate no data is being received.

You can do two things to test if the tracking code is in place.

1. Open a new tab in your browser and access the home page of site yourself by going to the domain. While on the site, go back to the browser tab that has the Google Analytics and click on the **Real-Time** link from the navigation. If tracking is installed you should

see an active user on the report shown on the screen.

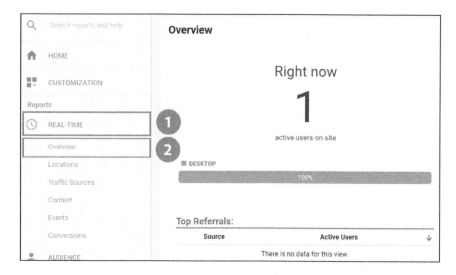

2. The second thing you can do to test if the tracking code is in place is to click the **Send Test Traffic** button found just under the **Status** section of the page.

If you find problems with your tracking code, you need to troubleshoot what the problem might be.

Troubleshooting Common Manual Install Tracking Issues

- **Is your tracking code in the right place on the site?** When you copy and paste the tracking code into your site or application, follow the instructions on the screen. Most often, the tracking code should be placed right after the opening <head> tag.

- **Wrong snippet used and/or you are viewing the wrong account, property, or view.** Make sure that you are using the correct code snippet (which would include the correct tracking ID) for the property you are tracking—especially if you are tracking multiple properties. Additionally, make sure you are viewing the reports for the same property that you installed the code on.

  Check the snippet by accessing your site in a browser and then clicking **View > Source** from the menu options. Search for the tracking code on the page and make sure the ID matches the ID of the property you are tracking.

- **Extra space or characters.** Copy the code exactly as you see it on the screen. Avoid copying the code snippet into a word processing program and then into your site. Word processing programs can often add extra spaces and formatting, which will render the code ineffective. If you must copy it into another source for any reason, using a simple text editor like Notepad works best.

- **Errors from customization.** Under certain circumstances you might want to customize the tracking code. When doing so, make sure you adhere to proper coding standards for best results.

- **Filter setting are incorrect.** Setting filters can affect the type of data you see in your reports. In fact, setting incorrect filters can remove all data from your reports. This most often happens when there are multiple include filters applied to the same view. If this is the case, go back and verify each of the filters to ensure proper setup.

- **Additional scripts on the page.** If there are any other scripts running on your page, make sure none of them conflicts with the Analytics variables. This gets a little more difficult to diagnose and may require your programmer/developer to debug.

Installation Option 2: Google Tag Manager

Google Tag Manager is a tag management system that allows you to easily add and update tracking snippets for a website or mobile app from within one convenient interface—even tracking codes from sources not related to Google. Although Tag Manager can be a little difficult to understand at first, I highly recommend using it if you have the opportunity.

Tag Manager has several benefits:

1. You'll have a complete overview of all the tags that are added to

your site, app, or device in one convenient location.

2. You no longer have to wait for a development team to add tracking code for you, then test it to make sure it's working. It saves time and put you in full control of measuring the effects of your marketing efforts.

The organizational structure of Tag Manager is similar to that of a Google Analytics account. You have accounts, and under that you have containers (similar to properties in Google Analytics), tags, and triggers. These elements relate to each other in the following way:

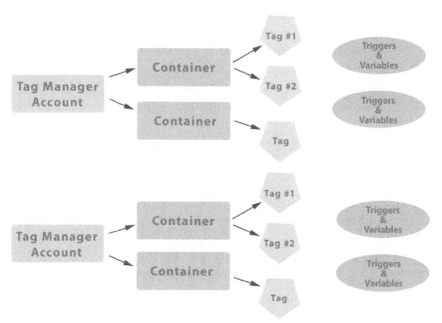

You can access Tag Manager from the drop-down on the Analytics login page, or go to **tagmanger.google.com**. You'll sign in using the same Google account you use for Analytics.

Setting Up Tag Manager

The basic steps for setting up Tag Manager are below. I'll cover each step in more detail following the list.

1. Create an account, or use an existing account, at tagmanager.google.com. In most cases, only one account is needed per company, and all tags for a company's content can be managed from this one account.

2. Create a new container for your website or mobile app and copy the tracking code snippet. Typically each container represents a different website you wish to track under one account.

3. Install the tracking code snippet on your site following the instructions on the screen.

    o For web pages: Add the container snippet to your site and

remove any existing tags.

    o For mobile apps: Use the Firebase SDK to implement Tag Manager.

4. Add, update, and publish tags.

Create a new account and container

1. In Tag Manager, click **Accounts > Setup Account**.

2. Enter an **Account Name**.

3. Click **Continue**.

4. Enter a descriptive container name and select the type of content: **Web, AMP, iOS**, or **Android**. If setting up a mobile container, select whether you're using the Firebase SDK or one of the legacy SDKs.

5. Click **Create**.

6. If required, accept the terms of service if you agree.

After creating your new container, you will be prompted with the installation code snippet, or you can get started with Tag Manager as part of the SDK for your chosen platform. Choose to install your code snippets now, or clear the dialog and install the snippet at a later date.

Add a new container to an existing account

In Google Tag Manager, click **Accounts** and then click the three dots next to the relevant account name.

- Choose **Create Container.**

- Repeat steps 4–6 listed above.

Install tracking code snippet on your site

1. From Tag Manager, click **Workspace**. At the top of the window, find your container ID, formatted as "GTM-XXXXXX."

2. Click the container ID to launch the **Install Google Tag Manager** box.

3. Follow the instructions on the screen to copy and paste the code snippets into your website, or download and install the appropriate mobile SDK.

4. Verify or troubleshoot your installation with Tag Manager's preview mode and the Tag Assistant Chrome extension.

Activate Google Analytics tag in Tag Manager

There are many different tags you can add once Tag Manager is set up. In this section I only focus on installing the basic Google Analytics script.

1. From the Tag Manager Workspace screen, click on **Add a New Tag.**

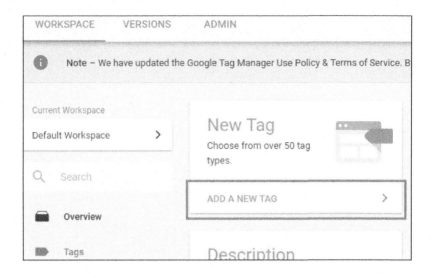

2. Give the new tag a name. In this example it's called Universal GA Tag.

3. Click anywhere in the **Tag Configuration** section to pull up the **Choose tag type** menu.

4. Choose **Universal Analytics** from the menu.

An example of these steps is shown in the image below.

After choosing the tag type, you need to set up the variable. Leave the **Track Type** set to **Page View** and choose **New Variable** from the **Google Analytic Settings** drop-down.

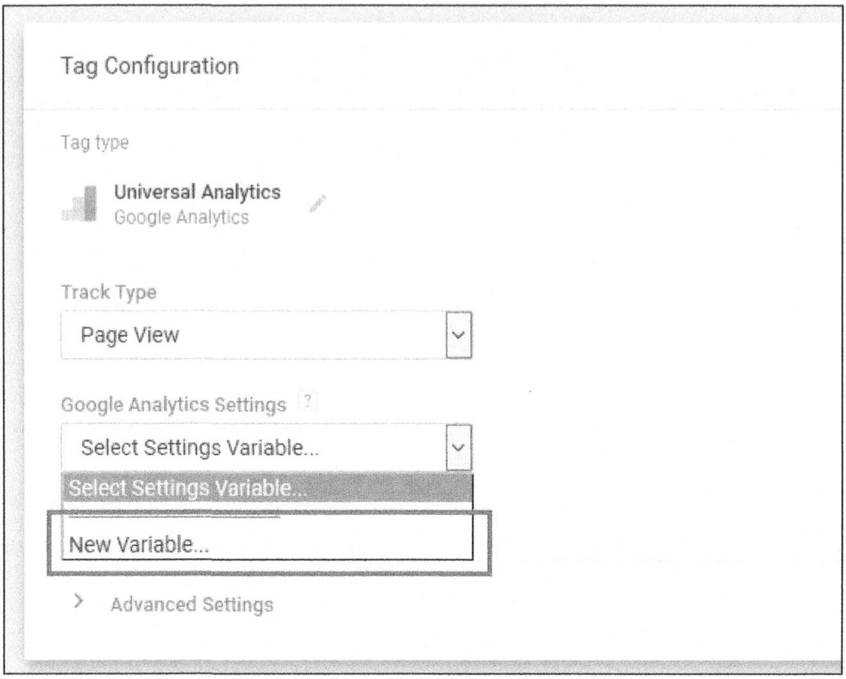

Tag Configuration

Tag type

Universal Analytics
Google Analytics

Track Type

Page View

Google Analytics Settings ?

Select Settings Variable...

Select Settings Variable...

New Variable...

> Advanced Settings

The next step is required to configure the variable for tracking.

Give the variable a name. In this example it's called "GA Universal ID."

Next add your Google Analytics tracking ID to the box provided. You can find your tracking ID (UA-XXXXX-X) using the same steps presented in the Installation Option 1: Manual Installation section above.

Google Analytics has some pretty powerful features, however in most cases you need to turn the features on in order to use them. So as an optional (yet recommended) feature, click on **More Settings**. Check **Enable Display Advertising Features,** and if you are an ecommerce site, check **Enable Enhanced Ecommerce Features,** as well.

Click **Save**.

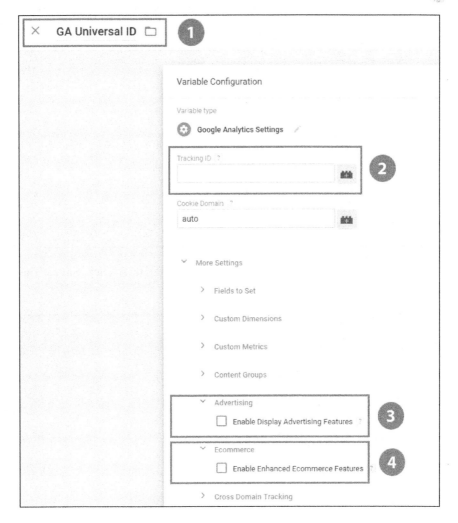

The final step is to set a trigger for firing this tag. To do this you need to go back to the **Tag Configuration** page and click anywhere in the area that says **Triggering**.

Choose **Page View** from the selection presented then click **Save.** The screen should now look similar to this:

Congratulations! You have now implemented Google Analytics universal tracking using Google Tag Manager.

Troubleshooting Common Tag Manager Tracking Issues

You can verify tracking code installation using the same steps presented in the Installation Option 1: Manual Installation section above. In the event there are problems, here are a few common troubleshooting areas to check:

- **Filter setting are incorrect.** Setting filters can affect the type of data you see in your reports. In fact, setting incorrect filters can remove all data from your reports. This most often happens when there are multiple include filters applied to the same view. If this is the case, go back and verify each of the filters to ensure proper setup.

- **Container not published.** Check to make sure you published your container after adding the Analytics tag. Additions or changes you make to a container do not go live on the site until you publish the container.

- **Tag not firing.** Go back and check the setting for when the tag is supposed to fire. In addition, make sure no other tracking codes on the page are conflicting with the firing.

What Type of Information Do Reports Include?

With "Vanilla" Google Analytics, you can expect to get reports on items you may be familiar with and have seen in other statistical reporting systems.

Some of that includes: new vs. returning visitors, unique vs. non-unique visits, browser types, pageviews, bounce rates, paid search vs. organic traffic sources, entry vs. exit pages, and more.

What You Can Learn From Tracking Results

The tracking results you obtain through "Vanilla" Google Analytics can provide you with information on your visitors, the traffic sources those visitors came from, the types of systems and technology they are using (such as browser types, screen resolutions, etc.), and how they travel through your site.

More importantly, the data can help you determine things like: which pages have the highest bounce rates, which search engines drive the most traffic, which keywords drive the most traffic, and more. Although a minor factor in determining conversion; these few bits of data can give you a hint of where you may have potential problems on your site that should be addressed, and help you determine how to best structure your site in order to get the most out of it.

Bounce Rates: A high bounce rate should be cause for concern, and needs to be addressed. After all, how can you expect a visitor to buy your product if the bounce rate for pages leading up to the sale is high? You can't, because they are never getting far enough to finish the sale!

The pages with the highest bounce rates should take priority over pages with lower bounce rates when making changes to increase the performance of your website. There is no reason to alter pages that have lower bounce rates until you address the issues of those that are causing problems.

On pages that have the highest bounce rates, take note of things like the position of elements on the page, the spelling and copy, the overall design of the page, the ease of use, the availability and ease of checkout, the presentation of the product itself (for ecommerce sites), the product description, the presence of customer assurances, and more.

Pay attention to pages where you present your prices and what offers you present to the user on those pages. Do you give customers the ability to continue confidently with the sale? Or are you making them think too much and pushing them away?

Oftentimes, understanding how your visitors search for and buy your product will enable you to address the changes needed to decrease bounce rates on your site.

Visitor Segmentation: On a broad scale, knowing where your visitors are coming from (which search engines, etc.) can also help you speak to them better. Certain engines have more of a male following, others female, and still others a mix. Knowing who your ideal customer is will help you speak to them in a way that will make them more inclined to purchase from you.

That is, if the product and price are right.

Keyword Popularity: Paying attention to the keywords and keyword phrases that users search to arrive at your site can greatly increase your conversion. Keywords can tell you how your visitors search for your product, what about your product is important to them, and where they expect to find information on that product, based on which page on your site they land on first.

Keyword searches can even help you uncover new product opportunities you may have not otherwise considered.

For example, If you notice that a large number of your visitors are arriving at your site on the word "Widgets" and you don't sell them, then you may want to consider offering them, or altering the page they are arriving to speak about how your product compares to a Widget (thus increasing the chances of them *not* leaving, but continuing further into your site).

If you sell only purple Widgets and you notice that a large portion of your visitors arrive at your site looking for blue Widgets, then you may want to consider adding blue as a new color option.

If you offer an on-site search feature, you should consider tracking the search terms entered there as well, using Google Analytics search tracking. More on this topic is covered in chapter 7.

3

ECOMMERCE TRACKING

What Is Ecommerce Tracking?

If you sell anything from your site, ecommerce tracking is a must. Google Analytics ecommerce tracking provides a means for recording data based on individual transactions that occur on your site. A single transaction typically represents one order. That order can be made up of one or more products.

Data from ecommerce tracking can include which products perform best, which generate the highest revenue amounts, what sources (paid search, organic search, etc.) the traffic came from that results in a purchased product, average order values, conversion rates, and more.

This is all valuable data that can be used for making sound business decisions, including how to approach your market with your products, where you may want to consider promoting them, and to whom.

Ecommerce Tracking Code

The tracking code for ecommerce is a completely separate snippet from what I call the "Vanilla" version. Although they are completely separate snippets, the ecommerce tracking requires basic Google Analytics tracking (i.e. "Vanilla") to be in place before it will work.

There are two options for tracking ecommerce transactions: standard ecommerce tracking and enhanced ecommerce tracking. Enhanced offers more reporting options than standard. I'll talk more about these shortly.

Regardless of the tracking version you choose, the ecommerce tracking code should be placed on the receipt page—typically the "thank you" page a visitor arrives at after making a successful sales transaction.

In addition, the ecommerce tracking code should be placed after the standard "Vanilla" Google Analytics tracking code. For this reason, it is often best to include this code at the bottom of your page in the footer.

Keep in mind that in order to start receiving accurate data on transactions, you will need to alter the code to include any dynamic variables provided by your shopping cart (replacing variables like [order-id], [affiliation], etc., with the proper variable from your cart to insert the dynamic values). This will require some degree of knowledge and understanding of your shopping cart's programming language. If you need assistance with this, consult your technical team.

How to Set Up Ecommerce Tracking

Setting up ecommerce tracking involves two main steps:

- Enable ecommerce reporting in Google Analytics.

- Add the ecommerce tracking code to your site or application.

The first step of tracking ecommerce transactions is to enable ecommerce reporting for each view in which you want to see data. If you do not do enable reporting, it won't matter if the tracking code is in place or not—you still will not receive any data. This is most often the problem when users have the ecommerce tracking code in place on their site but their analytic reports relating to ecommerce show no data.

To enable ecommerce reporting inside Google Analytics, follow these steps:

1. Log in to your Google Analytics account.

2. Click **Admin** (gear icon).

3. Click **Ecommerce Settings** under the view you want to enable ecommerce tracking for.

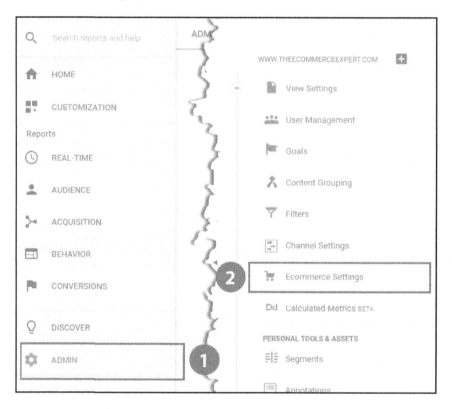

4. Enable the ecommerce setting by turning it **on**.

There are two types of ecommerce tracking methods:

Standard ecommerce tracking allows you to see product and transaction information, average order value, ecommerce conversion rate, time to purchase, and other data.

Enhanced ecommerce tracking extends the standard functionality by allowing you to see when customers have added items to their shopping carts, when they have started the checkout process, and when they have completed a purchase. It also allows you to identify where customers might be dropping out of the shopping funnel. For this reason, I recommend activating both options.

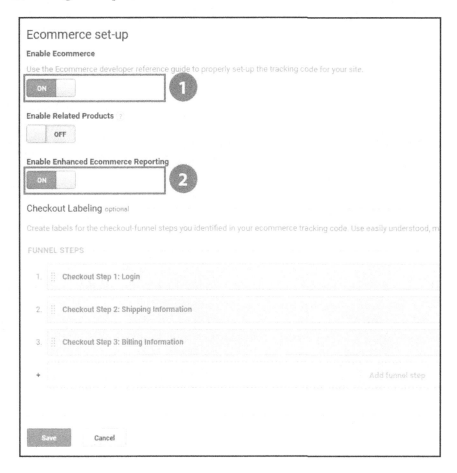

Understanding where bottlenecks are in the checkout can reduce cart abandons, keep users in the checkout process longer, and ultimately increase conversion rates.

To locate bottlenecks, set up a funnel that includes each step of the checkout process. It's best to name each step of the funnel something that indicates what it represents. An example representing the first three steps in a checkout process might be Checkout Step 1: Login; Checkout Step 2: Shipping Information; Checkout Step 3: Billing Information, etc. More on funnels is covered in chapter 6.

5. After activating the options and setting up funnels, click **Save.**

Now that ecommerce tracking has been enabled in Google Analytics, the second step in setting up ecommerce tracking is to ensure that the tracking code is included on the receipt page (i.e. "thank you" page after a sale).

Remember, Google ecommerce tracking requires that you *first* have the standard Google tracking code in place.

Placing the tracking code on the receipt page can be rather complicated, and the code can change from time to time as Google updates its product. As a result, I won't go into all the technical details involved, but I will touch upon a few brief things to be aware of when installing the code on your site.

Regardless of which option you choose (enhanced ecommerce or standard ecommerce tracking), start the code by loading the plugin from the Google server. This must occur after you create your tracker object and before you use any of the enhanced ecommerce specific functionality.

If you are using standard ecommerce tracking, load the plugin using the following code: **ga('require', 'ecommerce');**

If using enhanced ecommerce tracking, load the plugin using the following code: **ga('require', 'ec');**

NOTE: Load the plugin using only one of the two tags listed above. Adding both to a page will cause the tracking to fail.

Depending on which tracking method you used to install Google Analytics (manual installation or Google Tag Manager), the actual implementation of the ecommerce snippet can be complicated. In addition, the code changes often. So the best way to ensure you have the latest implementation code is to search Google for "google analytics ecommerce tracking." This search should provide plenty of direct links to Google's site with the latest code.

However, for illustrative purposes, an example of how the complete code might look for standard ecommerce follows:

```
<script>
ga('require', 'ecommerce');

ga('ecommerce:addTransaction', {
'id': '00123', // Transaction ID. Required.
'affiliation': 'Clothing Store', // Affiliation or store
name.
'revenue': '18.99', // Grand Total.
'shipping': '5', // Shipping.
'tax': '1.51' // Tax.
});

ga('ecommerce:addItem', {
'id': '00123', // Transaction ID. Required.
'name': 'Blue Tee Shirt', // Product name. Required.
'sku': 'ABC12345', // SKU/code.
'category': 'Women's Clothing', // Category or variation.
'price': '11.99', // Unit price.
'quantity': '1' // Quantity.
});

ga('ecommerce:send');
</script>
```

The code above should only be used as a structural reference; it is not intended to be a "copy and paste" illustration. Furthermore, the placement of code may differ depending on the type of code chosen.

For more technical information about how to implement the tracking code, see the following links based on your chosen method.

Standard ecommerce tracking implementation:

https://developers.google.com/analytics/devguides/collection/analyticsjs/ecommerce

Enhanced ecommerce tracking implementation:

https://developers.google.com/analytics/devguides/collection/analyticsjs/enhanced-ecommerce

Google Tag Manager ecommerce tracking implementation:

https://support.google.com/tagmanager/answer/6107169

Ecommerce Reporting

Once you have activated ecommerce tracking, you can access the reporting features.

If you activated the standard ecommerce tracking, you will find your report options under the **Conversions > Ecommerce** portion of your Analytics account.

Recall that with enhanced ecommerce tracking you get a number of added reporting features. As such, your menu options will change slightly.

If you activated the enhanced ecommerce tracking, you will find your report options under two areas within your Analytics account. The first section is still found under **Conversions > Ecommerce,** however, you'll see that a few new options are now listed under that area. The second reporting option can be accessed just under the ecommerce section by going to **Conversions > Marketing.**

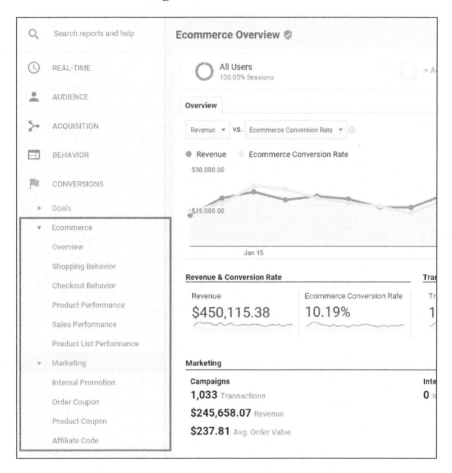

What Information Do Reports Contain?

With Google Analytics ecommerce tracking, you can expect to get reports on items that relate directly to transactions (sales) occurring on the site.

Depending on which version you activated (standard or enhanced), your report options will differ. However, in general, you can expect reports to include data such as: top revenue sources by product, top revenue sources by referring engine, which keywords generate the most sales revenue, average order value, which categories generate the most revenue, what traffic sources generate the most revenue, how promotions and coupons affect sales, conversion rate, and more.

What You Can Learn From Tracking Results

Activating ecommerce tracking opens new doors to learning what drives revenue and what doesn't. You'll learn how individual products perform and what the top products are. With enhanced ecommerce tracking, you also get valuable marketing information including which coupons and sales produce the best response rates along with shopping and checkout behavior of customers.

You'll receive a wealth of information from the reports available through ecommerce tracking. I'll cover a few metrics and features you'll want to pay attention to. These metrics and features provide a solid foundation for decision making that helps increase conversion, but keep in mind they are only a starting point.

Ecommerce Overview report:

Revenue & Conversion Rate		Transactions	
Revenue	Ecommerce Conversion Rate	Transactions	Avg. Order Value
$441,593.36	8.06%	1,835	$240.65

Use this report to see average order values, conversion rate, and total revenue.

Product Performance: This report lets you analyze performance of individual products. The report offers two perspectives on product performance.

Summary	Shopping Behavior
• Revenue generated by product	• Product views in a list
• Quantity sold	• Product-detail views

• Average price	• Product adds to cart
• Refund amounts	• Product removals from cart
• Cart-to-detail ratio	• Number of times product was included in checkout
• Buy-to-detail ratio	• Unique purchases
	• Cart-to-detail ratio
	• Buy-to-detail ratio

In addition to reporting on revenue and quantity figures, this report provides an indicator of how well your site design leads to conversions. You'll find this information in the Shopping Behavior view which is covered shortly in this chapter.

Top Revenue Sources: Top Revenue Sources tells you where the visitors who buy your product(s) come from. This is important data that should help you determine where to focus your marketing efforts, and where you need to improve them.

This data can also help you determine the search behavior of your ideal customer. For example, if most of your visitors come from the Google search engine, then chances are they make decisions quickly based upon what they want. (Google's search interface gets straight to the point and offers very little distraction to its users.) On the other hand, if most of your traffic comes from Bing or Yahoo, then your users may need a little more information to provoke them to buy (like more detailed product descriptions).

This is not a methodology that is set in stone—search engines and the demographics of people who use them change often—much depends on the market segment to which you are selling, but it can be a theory deduced from current analysis of user search habits.

So, let's go back and say your reports indicate that Google organic search traditionally provides the most revenue for your store. Then you may want to target that traffic channel more by increasing your exposure there, which could result in more sales. However, you may prefer to target a weaker traffic segment to gain more sales from that as well and only maintain the Google organic channel for sustained sales.

Likewise, if one channel provides more profit than another, you may want to dig deeper to find out why and target similar traffic channels for more exposure.

The thing to keep in mind is, *all traffic is not created equal* and traffic channels will drive visitors with distinctly different demographics, wants, and needs. Target your ideal customer, segment your visitors, speak to them from a buyer's perspective and give them just the right amount of information they need to make the sale.

Top Revenue Sources by Product: When you add ecommerce tracking to Google Analytics, it can create a Top Revenue Sources by Product report. There are a number of ways to utilize the data gathered from this metric. One idea would be to take the top revenue generating products and feature them on the home page or prominent locations throughout your site.

You already know through reporting that these products are purchased most often and generate most of your revenue, so putting them directly in front of visitors arriving at your site eliminates the extra clicks that typically increase abandonment rates.

You'll be making it even easier for them to find the product and add it to their cart. Your sales should reflect this change.

Another strategy might be to showcase a few products with higher profit margins but lower revenue figures. Bringing these products to the front of the mix could generate higher sales and larger margins.

Average Order Value: Average order value is the average total transaction amount of each order placed from your site. The figure takes all orders for the given period of time analyzed and then averages the total amount of all those orders to arrive at the final number.

Many ecommerce sites monitor this metric to see if cross promotions are working. Why? Because when you cross promote products properly, the amount a customer spends at your store increases, and in turn the average order value increases.

In short, the average order value is the average total amount an individual customer spends during his or her visit to your store. Increasing this number means you are putting additional revenue in your pocket.

Take note of your current average order value. Your ability to increase it will greatly add to your ability to increase total sales revenue.

How can you increase your average order value? That is up to you, but a few examples are:

1. Increasing the product prices at your store.

2. Creating bundles of multiple products that, when combined, increase the amount a customer spends at your store.

3. Creating free shipping incentives for order amounts over a certain threshold. Increasing the amount needed to qualify for free shipping will naturally increase your average order value.

4. Adding new products to your store with higher product prices.

5. Upsell higher-end products that are similar to the one being considered. If you offer multiple versions of similar products at different price points, upselling to the higher-end product can sometimes increase your average order value.

6. Cross-selling one product with another related product. The two combined, when purchased, will increase the average order value.

Take careful note: Setting up cross-sells between products just for the sake of cross-selling is not as effective as setting up cross-sells between actual **related** products or accessories.

As I see it, there are two types of cross-sell techniques. One is more effective at increasing average order values than the other.

The automated cross-sell looks at what is in the customer's cart and compares that with other customers who purchased the same product. It then presents the user with a list of items and often is titled "customers who bought this product also purchased."

Does it work? Sure, to some extent it gets things right...sometimes. Take for example, the shopper at an online department store like Amazon. She purchases a bicycle and helmet for her child along with some elbow pads. Before she checks out, she adds a TV to the cart and completes the sale.

Another visitor to Amazon comes along looking for a new TV and compatible components. He finds a TV and adds it to his cart. Upon adding the item to his cart, he gets an automated cross-sell that promotes a kid's bicycle, helmet, and elbow pads stating "customers who bought this product also purchased this."

If the TV buyer has no kids, and isn't interested in that type of offer, the cross-sell fails due to lack of relevancy.

The manual cross-sell requires human intervention to match up compatible products with each other instead of letting a machine determine what to offer. More control means more targeted cross-sells and an increased opportunity to bump average order values.

Using the above example, with a little human intervention, the person searching for a TV without children could be presented with additional electronic components that not only make more sense, but are fully compatible with the TV he is considering.

As that customer adds the TV to his cart, with manual cross-selling, he is presented with a surround sound stereo receiver, a universal remote control, and even batteries for the remote control. Furthermore, the title of the cross-sell section is labeled "complementary items that complete the package."

Whether the customer adds the items to his cart or not, this cross-sell provides far more relevancy to his interests and as such, presents a better opportunity to increase the average order value.

To illustrate the point further, I provide two final examples of good vs. bad cross-sells below.

- A good cross promotion, and one that could increase sales, would be cross-selling batteries to a customer who is purchasing a flashlight.

- A bad cross promotion would be cross-selling batteries to a customer who is purchasing a garden shovel.

The important thing to remember when considering a cross-selling strategy is that testing is always a good idea. Every business is different and what works for one won't always work for another. In fact, it might be a good idea to test using both automated and manual options on the same page. I would put the manual (more relevant) option first and then, lower on the page, test the inclusion of the automated option. Gather results of the testing and use what combination works best.

Speaking of cross-selling and promotions, the Product List Performance report provides information on how effective your on-site marketing efforts are.

Product List Performance: This report shows how individual products perform together when presented within various listings. It provides information on the product lists you choose to show visitors to illustrate product options, upsells, cross-sells, and related products. This is powerful data that can be used to make even more refined lists in an effort to increase conversion and average order values.

Set the primary dimension to **Product List Name** if seeking data analysis from a list perspective. Each list shows the number of times it was viewed, the number of times an item from the list was clicked, and the click-through rate. These metrics are used as indicators to determine how well a list performs at getting products in front of visitors and whether the layout, text, and graphics persuade visitors to click for more detailed information.

Set the primary dimension to **Product List Position** to find out which position performs best for a list.

Set the primary dimension to **Product** if you are interested in seeing how individual products perform within the lists they appear on.

Taking this a step further, let's combine two of the above options. Keep **Product** as the primary dimension and then set **Product List Position** as the secondary dimension. This report now shows how individual products perform relative to their list position. If you notice that a lower position product is outperforming one that is in a higher position in the list, consider moving that better-performing product to a higher spot on the list.

Coupon & Sales Performance: Under the marketing option for ecommerce reporting, you'll find features that provide information on how well your on-site promotions work to drive conversion.

This includes information for site-wide and individual product coupon codes (offers) as well as any promotional campaigns you may run.

You'll find product-specific data relating to overall revenue earned from a coupon code, average product revenue for each purchase that included a given coupon code, and the number of unique purchases that included the coupon code. In addition, data is presented that shows the average order value for all transactions associated with a coupon.

Use the information discovered in the reporting to plan future promotional efforts around the most successful campaigns, messages, and coupon offers.

Shopping Behavior Analysis:

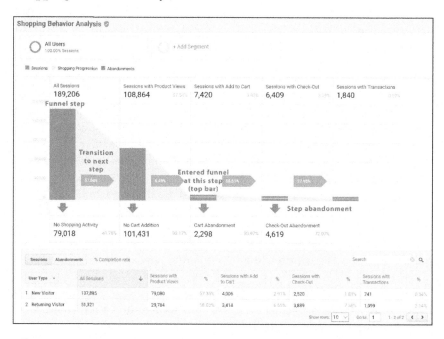

The Shopping Behavior Analysis report details how effective your purchase funnel is at converting visitors to sales. How often did the design of the product listing pages encourage visitors to view a single product? How well does the site design lead visitors to individual product detail pages, get the visitor to add an item to the cart, and ultimately complete the purchase?

In its simplest form, the Shopping Behavior Analysis report shows the number of sessions that make up each stage of your purchase funnel, how many sessions continued to the next step, and how many abandoned at each stage.

The red arrows are points at which a user abandoned the process and did not complete any more steps during the same session. A user can later reenter the funnel at any step (indicated by the top portion of blue bar at any given step.) One example of how this might happen is if a user adds something to her cart and then leaves the site. She comes back at a later date (starting a new session) and begins the process again. The funnel process would count that user as reentering the funnel at the next step from the one where she left during the prior session.

You can further segment this data to get a more granular data view of users that fit your specific criteria. Google creates steps based upon the tagging you set within your ecommerce tracking code.

Use this report to identify barriers and weaknesses within your purchase funnel. Some helpful hints of what to look for and how to possibly address each situation are listed below:

- If you notice an unusually high abandonment rate at any step, take a close look at the content on that page.

- If you find that visitors are viewing product details but not adding items to their cart, it might be that the product descriptions are not compelling enough, don't provide enough detail, or have the wrong information for them to make a buying decision. Remember earlier in the book when I mentioned understanding your customer and targeting them properly? This is a good time to revisit that information.

  For example, if your target customer is the typical mainstream consumer and your descriptions are full of technical jargon, it may not appeal to them enough to add the item to their cart. On the other hand, a "copy and paste" product description from a manufacturer might provide too little information and not resonate with them either. Finding the right mix is the key to success.

Viewing product details and not adding an item to the cart could even mean customer confidence builders and assurances are missing from the product page. When present, these typically put the customer at ease by answering questions they have at various points in the buying cycle. In the case of the product page, before a visitor adds an item to his cart he asks questions such as, "What methods of payment are available if I add this item to my cart?" "Is my transaction secure?" "If I don't like the product can I return it easily?" "Are there any guarantees?" or "What are my shipping options?" If answers to these questions are not at the point of action (POA) the chances of getting the visitor to move to the next step are greatly reduced.

And finally, if visitors are viewing descriptions and not adding items to their cart, it could mean there is a technical glitch preventing them from doing so. All avenues must be addressed to find the answer.

- If visitors are adding items to their cart and then leaving, a few things may be happening. They may be comparison-shopping to find out which retailer is going to offer them the best incentive to complete the order. Keep up with what your competitors are doing to ensure you are able to counter any current incentives they offer if necessary.

  Those visitors might also be looking for shipping information (timeframe of delivery and rates). Don't make potential customers wait to find out what it will cost to ship their order until they are in the checkout process. That's a sure remedy for high abandonment rates. Instead, offer them the ability to calculate shipping directly from the shopping cart page—before they ever start the checkout process.

- If you find visitors abandoning the purchase process at the checkout, it could be caused by a number of factors, including missing customer assurance factors at the POA, a process that is too complicated, a process that is not well-designed, or something else. Testing is the key to solving this issue, and the next report we look at helps uncover precisely *where* in the checkout process you might have problems.

Checkout Behavior Analysis:

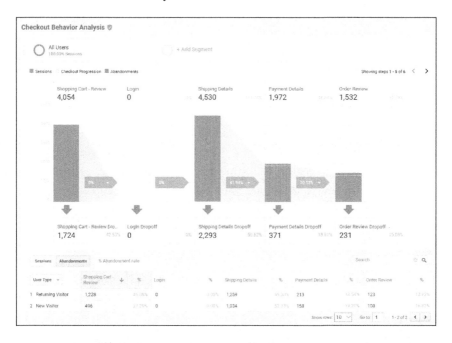

Where the Shopping Behavior Analysis report details the effectiveness of the steps leading up to the start of the checkout process, the Checkout Behavior Analysis report details how effective your checkout process is at converting visitors who enter it into sales.

From this report, you can discover areas of weakness and barriers to purchase at each step within the checkout process. Finding and correcting them helps decrease abandonment and increase conversion.

For example, if you require users to log in as the first step of the checkout process, and notice a lot of them dropping out at that stage, you might want to consider adding a guest checkout option. Even with that option, you might still notice higher than expected abandonment at that page.

Take a close look at the design. Is it optimized for ease of use? Have you presented them with enough customer assurances to make them feel comfortable to continue? Are the instructions on how to proceed and what they can expect when they do clear and evident?

If you offer multiple steps in the checkout process and you find visitors leaving at the shipping step, it could be that the rates are higher than they like or that the options for shipping are not as abundant as they would like.

Abandonment at the payment stage might signal a lack of customer assurances at the POA (on the payment page, those assurances are very important near the area where they enter the credit card information), lack of security features, or a lack of payment options.

In a multi-step process, when a customer reaches the order confirmation page the abandonment should be virtually nothing. If you find any abandonment at this stage, check the wording of the page. Do the page titles and buttons make it feel like the sale has already completed? This is often the case when the title of the page is worded similar to "Order Confirmation" and the button to complete the order is worded "Confirm Order."

This can be confusing to a customer. Typically, abandons at this stage are because customers are led to believe they have already completed the order and are at the order confirmation screen. In fact, there is one more step in the process. Changing the way the page is worded can help remedy this problem in most cases.

Finally, as was the case with the Shopping Behavior Analysis, an unusually high number of abandons at any step might indicate a technical glitch that needs to be corrected.

In the end, there is no better method to incrementally increase conversion and decrease abandons than to conduct usability testing across the entire process.

4

CONVERSION TRACKING

What Is Conversion Tracking?

Conversion tracking reports on the types of actions a customer takes when engaging with your website or application. Purchasing a product on your site, joining a newsletter, filling out a contact form, calling your business, and downloading your app are all examples of types of actions that can be tracked with conversion tracking.

The key metric reported on from conversion tracking is conversion rate. Recall from chapter 1 that conversion rate measures how well your website or application turns visitors into leads or sales. In other words, conversion rate is the percentage of users who take a desired action on your site or app.

There are several ways you can track conversion within Google Analytics. I cover some of the most common ways in this guide. The first is conversion tracking as it relates to goals. The second is conversion tracking as it relates to ecommerce transactions, and the third area is conversion tracking as it relates to Google Ads (I cover this in chapter 5).

If you look at any Google Analytics reports or dashboards you might notice several areas where conversion rate is reported and each area doesn't always equal the same number. This is because conversion rate can be tracked for various actions including items such as contact us form submissions, online sales, and phone calls just to name a few.

Both report on essentially the same metric, however they get their data in different ways. Therefore it is entirely possible to have an ecommerce conversion rate of 1 percent, yet a goal conversion rate of 2 percent. The setup of each determines how and what it reports on.

When you install and activate Google Analytics ecommerce tracking, you'll automatically be able to track the conversion rate as it relates to ecommerce transactions. Details on that were covered in the previous chapter. However, conversion rate as it relates to goals requires a bit more setup.

What Are Goals?

Goals measure how well your site or application meets target objectives. If this sounds familiar, it should because a goal tracks conversions, resulting in a conversion rate metric that is a measure of the same. Goals represent completed actions within your site or application. Examples might be shopping cart sales and contact us form submissions.

Goal tracking is a lot like ecommerce tracking, however it doesn't provide the level of detail that ecommerce tracking adds. Whereas ecommerce tracking is typically reserved for ecommerce sites, goal tracking can be used for both ecommerce and non-ecommerce related sites.

It is the method of choice for measuring conversion when ecommerce tracking is not an option, and is even run as an additional method when ecommerce tracking *is* an option.

If your website is designed to drive visitors to a particular page, such as a purchase "thank you" page or email sign-up page, you can track the number of successful conversions using goals and funnels in Google Analytics. It is even possible to use goals for tracking add to cart actions and time on site actions that don't lead the visitor to a particular page.

Example of Goals You May Want to Track

- Shopping cart sale (receipt confirmation page)

- Contact request

- Free downloads

- Newsletter sign up

- Completing a game level (in mobile gaming apps)

- Time spent on a particular page (indicates content consumption)

- Add-to-cart actions

How to Set Up Goal Tracking

Goals are configured at the view level of an account and can be tagged with a monetary value or left at a zero value. Assigning a monetary value to a goal helps define which goals add more value to the business.

For ecommerce stores, using a dynamic value equal to the order total is a recommended practice. For lead-generation type goals (i.e. contact us forms for a service type business), assign the value based on a percentage of sales closed by your internal team. Example: If your sales team closes 30 percent of all prospects that arrive from a contact form, and your average sale is $400 then you might assign a $120 value to the goal related to each form submission.

Follow these steps to set up goal tracking within Google Analytics:

1. From the Admin section of analytics, click **Goals** for the view you want to add the goal to.

2. Click **+New Goal.**

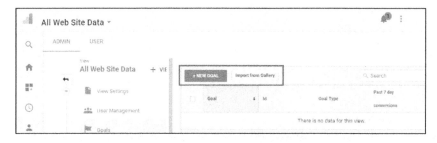

3. Choose your goal template. In this example I'm using the goal for a completed order as my template. This is common for tracking sales on ecommerce sites.

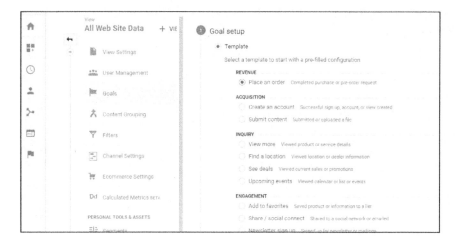

4. Name the goal and choose the type of goal. For most ecommerce transactions this will be a destination.

5. Complete the goal details section and save it. Turn the **Value** field on and enter the value of each conversion. (If tracking dynamic values such as those that come from ecommerce transactions, you'll want to alter the code once it is generated to replace the value you enter here with the proper syntax your shopping cart requires.)

If you want to track the effectiveness of the sales funnel leading up to this goal, then turn the **Funnel** on (funnels are covered in depth in chapter 6.) You can always add a funnel to an existing goal later on if desired.

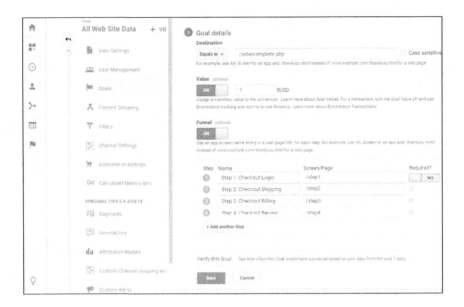

Destination URL Considerations

Fixed URLs

A fixed URL is one that remains the same and doesn't change. Examples of fixed URLs are:

http://www.somedomain.com/furniture/outdoor.php
http://www.somedomain.com/furniture/diningroom.html
http://www.somedomain.com/thank-you.php

To configure goals for fixed URLs, first ensure that the URL is completely unique to that page/goal and consistent from view to view. If the URL changes at all, then it is considered dynamic, and needs to be configured differently (more on this in the section labeled dynamic URLs.)

If the URL is the same across multiple steps in the goal process, see Identical URLs Across Multiple Steps (below). If the URL changes from view to view, or if it has name/value parameters, see the instructions for dynamically generated URLs.

Once it has been determined that the page is unique, use each of the following sections to complete the goal setup:

Destination: Enter only the request URI into this field. This is the portion of the URL that is after the domain name. Make sure to include the initial forward slash (without the initial slash tracking may not work). In the examples listed, the URI entered would be:

/furniture/outdoor.php
/furniture/diningroom.html
/thank-you.php

Case Sensitive: Be careful with this option and only use it when you want to distinguish between two identical URLs that only differ by case (Example: /THANKYOU.php and thankyou.php).

Match Type: Choose the match type that fits your needs. More information on match types is covered below.

Value: As mentioned earlier, if you want to track the value of goal (for ecommerce transactions this would be the order total) enter that value here. For contact form submissions that don't lead to a sale, you might leave this at zero.

If you know the value of your goal and it never changes, enter that number here. If on the other hand that value is dynamic (i.e. changes), as is the case with an ecommerce store, you may want to enter a temporary value here. You'll need to find that value in the tracking code that is produced and then change it to insert the dynamic value according to your shopping cart requirements.

Dynamic URLs

If the URL you set the goal for changes on a frequent basis or has query parameters appended to it, choose either **Begins with** or **Regular Expression** match types. Examples of dynamic URLs are:

http://www.somedomain.com/furniture/outdoor.php?pid=174

http://www.somedomain.com/furniture/diningroom.php?page=product&pid=378

Identical URLs

In certain circumstances the URL might not change across the entire sequence of activity. This often is the case when AJAX is being used in the application. In those instances, for example in the case of a checkout process controlled by AJAX, the checkout might have the following URL path:

Step 1: Checkout Information
(http://www.somedomain.com/checkout.php)

Step 2: Shipping Method
(http://www.somedomain.com/checkout.php)

Step 3: Payment Method
(http://www.somedomain.com/checkout.php)

Step 4: Checkout Processing
(http://www.somedomain.com/checkout.php)

Step 5: Order Complete
(http://www.somedomain.com/checkout.php) *Step 5 would essentially be the end goal in the process.*

There are two ways of handling this. The first method (which may be the easiest) is to use Event Tracking. In other words, setting up an event goal instead of a destination goal. When event tracking is used, there usually are no resulting funnel visualization reports that can be read. Instead, the data gathered must be pieced together in a different section of Google Analytics reporting.

For more advanced users and nicer funnel visualization, modify the tracking code provided by Google to trigger a virtual pageview for each step in the process. This method requires understanding of code or a programming team that can do it for you. An example of the type of tracking code modifications that would need to be made for this to occur are as follows:

```
ga('send','pageview','/checkout/contact_information');
ga('send','pageview',' /checkout/shipping');
ga('send','pageview',' /checkout/payment');
ga('send','pageview',' /checkout/checkout_processing');
ga('send','pageview','/checkout/thank_you'); (this is the completed goal)
```

The resulting goal details for tracking each step in the process with the modifications would look like the following:

Goal Match Types

If you choose URL Destination as your goal type, one of the additional options you must set is called a match type. Currently there are three different match types offered—**Equals to, Begins with,** and **Regular Expression.** Be careful when selecting which match type to use, as these are what Google Analytics uses to identify a URL for a goal or a funnel.

What Is the Difference Between Match Types?

Equals to: Equals to requires that the URLs entered as your funnel *and* goal URLs exactly match the URLs shown in your analytics reports. This means there can be *no* dynamic content identifiers or query string parameters. Under some circumstances, exact matches may also be regular expressions.

An example of what would be considered a dynamic identifier is seen highlighted in bold in the URL below:

http://www.yourdomain.com/index.php**?main_page=product_info&cP ath=14&products_id=3**

HELPFUL HINT

If you are using exact match for a goal (for example, *http://www.yourdomain.com/somepage.html*), any trailing spaces will cause the goal to be invalid. If you are using partial matching (for example: *^/page.html*), trailing spaces are not an issue.

Begins with: If your website has dynamically generated content but the base URL being tracked remains the same, use the Begins with filter and leave out the unique values.

For example, if the URL for a particular page is http://www.yourdomain.com/index.php?main_page=product_info&cPath =14&products_id=3 but the "cPath" and "products_id" varies for every other user, select Begins with as your match type and enter the URL http://www.yourdomain.com/index.php?main_page=product_info.

Regular Expression: This option uses regular expressions to match your URLs. A regular expression is a string that is used to describe or match a set of strings, according to certain syntax rules. This can be useful when the stem, trailing parameters, or both vary between visitors.

If a visitor might be coming from one of many subdomains or URLs within your domain, and your URLs use session identifiers, then you can use regular expressions to define the constant element of your URL for matching purposes.

For example, *main_page=product_info* will match the following URL

http://yourdomain.com/index.php**?main_page=product_info**&cPath=1

4&products_id=3

as well as

http://www.yourdomain.com/index.php?**main_page=product_info**&cPath=18&products_id=50

and even

http://widgets.yourdomain.com/index.php?**main_page=product_info**&sesid=agwe1726fhq63h

With Regular Expression these match, even though all three URLs are actually different.

Verifying Correct URL Expressions for Goals

Regular expressions are not easy to work with and can be confusing if you're not familiar with them. There are a number of free tools on the internet that will help you build a regular expression for use in Google Analytics.

One way to verify if you have written a goal URL correctly is to search for that URL in the pages report using the exact URL or regular expression you created. If the page you expect is returned, then you can be pretty confident that the expression you are using will work.

Examples:

Begins with

Imagine an ecommerce site that sells different types of furnishings. You want to set up a Begins with match URL goal to track the products in the rustic category only. The rustic category contains various products with a URL structure similar to:

/furniture/rustictables.php
/furniture/rusticbenches.php
/furniture/rusticmediacenters.php

To test whether the URI works, navigate to the All Pages report, click on the **Advanced** button, choose **Include, Page,** and **Begins with** for the search field. In the search field enter /furniture/rustic. If the results returned are the pages you expected to match, you can then use that same URI search string for the goal URL.

Regular Expression

You can test your regular expressions using the same All Pages report but entering your regular expression into the search field.

Take the furniture store example again. The store groups many of its products into collections with each collection a mixture of the products. The site has a number of pages that use collections as part of the file path:

http://www.somedomain.com/furniture/collections/backwoods/tables
http://www.somedomain.com/furniture/collections/home/tables
http://www.somedomain.com/collections/aspen/tables
http://www.somedomain.com/collections/barnwood/benches
http://www.somedomain.com/furniture/backwoodscollections.php

If wanting to set up a goal that triggers when any of the collection pages are viewed, you need to use a regular expression because not all of the collections are under the same directory.

Using the All Pages report in the Behavior Reporting section, enter .*collection[^/]*html$ into the search box. Verify your expression works by looking at the returned files in the report and making sure all of them contain the word "collections" as part of the name and no other files.

If everything looks correct, you can confidently use this same regular expression as the URL for the goal or funnel you are setting up.

Tracking Goals on Third-Party Sites

To track goals on third-party sites, the Google Analytics tracking code needs to be in place on the third-party site. Unfortunately, this isn't always an option. Under those circumstances where you would like to track goals on an external third-party site but do not have control over the code on that site (example: an ecommerce store transfers the customer to PayPal to complete the order) you can track the *outbound link* as a goal or funnel step.

You would do this by adding additional tracking code to the site similar to the following:

```
<script>
/**
* Function that tracks a click on an outbound link in
Analytics.
* This function takes a valid URL string as an argument,
and uses that URL string
* as the event label. Setting the transport method to
'beacon' lets the hit be sent
* using 'navigator.sendBeacon' in browser that support it.
*/
var trackOutboundLink = function(url) {
    ga('send', 'event', 'outbound', 'click', url, {
      'transport': 'beacon',
      'hitCallback': function(){document.location = url;}
    });
}
</script>
```

For this to work, You will also need to update the code on your link to include an onclick event for the element you want to track:

```
<a href="http://www.thirdpartydomain.com"
onclick="trackOutboundLink('http://www.thirdpartydomain.com
'); return false;">Pay with ThirdPartyDomain</a>
```

The code above will generate outbound link reporting that can be found in the Analytics Events report with a category of "outbound," action of "click," and the URL of the site the visitor was transferred to.

.

What Type of Information Do Reports Include?

With Google Analytics goals in place, you can expect to get information on how often visitors reach the goals you set forth in your website or application. You'll get reports on conversion rates, total conversions, total conversion value, and more.

What You Can Learn From Tracking Goals

Once you have set your goals, you'll be able to report on conversion rates and the monetary value of the traffic you receive in much the same way as you would with ecommerce tracking or Google Ads conversion tracking in place. (Google Ads conversion tracking is covered later in this guide.)

The information received from goal tracking can help you discover strengths and weaknesses of your website or application with regard to how well it meets your business objectives. A poorly performing goal indicates an area of weakness that needs to be looked at closely.

As important as goals are, alone they serve mainly to report on basic key performance indicators (KPIs) relating to the business. However, to get even greater reporting capabilities from goals, you can define a funnel. A funnel is the path a visitor takes to reach a particular goal. Defining a funnel allows you to monitor how frequently visitors who begin your assigned conversion process complete it or abandon it.

5

FUNNELS

What Are Funnels?

Some conversion goals—like those arrived at after a successful purchase—are preceded by pages used to drive the visitor toward that goal. These preceding pages can be looked at as the funnel. In other words, funnels are specific paths a visitor takes during the conversion process that lead up to a single goal.

Funnel tracking is used to determine how effectively you retain visitors throughout that conversion process. This tracking helps you pinpoint and target problem areas at any point during the process so meaningful efforts can be taken to improve conversion.

In order to set up a funnel in Google Analytics, you must first set up a goal.

Tips for Setting Up Funnels

All destination URL goals also provide you the option to set up a funnel associated with that goal.

When setting up a funnel, keep in mind the following points:

- Run through the entire process that leads to your goal on your website or application yourself and make note of the URL for all pages that are part of it. For sites where the URL doesn't change from step to step (like those often seen in AJAX driven ecommerce checkouts) make note of the pages and then prepare to alter tracking code using the same virtual pageview technique discussed in chapter 4 in the "Identical URLs" section.

- The final page in the process represents the actual goal. (For an ecommerce site this might be the "thank you" page after a successful checkout.) The URL for this page should be entered in the destination field, not as the last step in the funnel portion.

- The match type you select when setting up the goal is the same match type that will be used for each of the URLs in the funnel so make sure those are entered according to the rules of that match type.

- To avoid any potential issues with tracking, it is best to remove the domain name from each of the URLs you use in the funnel steps. (Example: http://www.somedomain.com/step1 should be entered as /step1.) If you choose to set the first step of the funnel as a required step, then only those visitors who reach that step before continuing on will be counted toward the final numbers in the Visualization report.

- To further clarify: If a visitor enters the funnel at step two, but then at some point visits step one, that visitor will be counted toward the conversions in the funnel Visualization report. If however, the visitor enters at step two of the process and then proceeds to the final conversion step without ever visiting step one, then that visitor will be excluded from conversion reporting on the funnel Visualization report.

   NOTE: This pertains to the funnel Visualization report only. It does not affect conversion reporting within any other report.

Ideally, when you set up a funnel, the visitor starts at the beginning of the funnel, and ends with the goal associated with that funnel. However, this sequence_ of actions is not always followed.

Visitors who start the process and do not complete it in its entirety from beginning to end are said to have abandoned the process. For ecommerce sites tracking a funnel through the checkout process, this is often considered shopping cart abandonment. Taking measures to reduce this behavior requires careful analysis and testing of each point in the funnel where the abandonment is occurring.

How to Set Up (Define) Funnels

Setting up a funnel, also called defining a funnel, can be achieved as follows:

1. Open a previously defined destination goal or create a new one and turn on the funnel option.

2. Enter the URL of the first page of your conversion funnel. This should be a page that is common to all users working their way toward your goal. For example, if you are tracking user flow through your checkout pages, do not include a product page as a step in your funnel.

3. Enter a name for this step.

4. If this step is a required step in the conversion process, select the checkbox to the right of the step. If this checkbox is selected, users reaching your goal page without traveling through this funnel page will not be counted as conversions.

5. Continue entering goal steps until your funnel has been completely defined. You may enter as many steps as needed, or as few as a single step.

6. Once you complete the funnel, click **Save** to finish.

Verify the funnel is working by looking at the funnel Visualization report. The image below shows what the final result might look like.

What Type of Information Do Reports Include?

A funnel represents the path that you expect visitors to take in order to reach a desired goal.

Defining this path allows you to see how frequently visitors abandon goals, where they go when they abandon, and the total conversion rate of how effectively your funnel achieves your goal objective.

A partial sample funnel Visualization report is shown on the next page for reference.

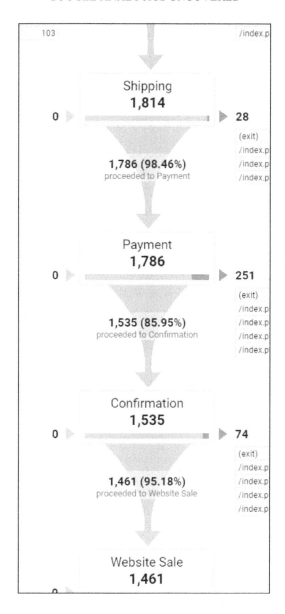

What Can You Learn From Funnel Reports?

Creating funnels helps you map out a pre-determined path that you want your visitors to travel down in order to reach the end goal. This path ideally should consist of elements that are pertinent to the end result, and that continually increase customer confidence and persuade them to act upon that confidence.

The information gathered through reports can shed light on weaknesses within your site that need attention. Areas that cause abandonment rates to jump should be carefully analyzed. Deductions should be made, and plans of action put into place to improve them.

When assigned to a checkout process, information provided by funnel tracking can be vital to increasing sales. Determine where your visitors abandon the process then analyze the page(s) for clues to help you understand why.

In addition, properly developed funnels can help you determine if the products you offer are the problem, or if how you present them is.

Let's say your funnel reports show visitors leaving the site at your product pages. You run tests on those pages but abandonment doesn't decrease. Then you may want to look at expanding the products you offer or determine if you are speaking to or targeting the proper market.

There is no set-in-stone answer to these issues, and each market is different. The important thing to remember is that a thorough analysis of properly set up funnels can reveal information that otherwise would be hidden. What that information tells you determines where you need to focus your efforts toward improving your conversion process.

Oftentimes testing is required to find the solution to abandonment. Begin by changing those pages that have highest abandonment rates and work your way to better-performing pages from there.

6

GOOGLE ADS CONVERSION TRACKING

What Is Google Ads Conversion Tracking?

So far I've covered conversion tracking within Google Analytics as it relates to both ecommerce transactions and to goals. Even though Google reports on those two types of conversion rates, there is yet another type of conversion tracking it can report on.

This conversion tracking measures how effective online advertising campaigns are—specifically those that are run through Google Ads.

Google Ads conversion tracking measures how effective your pay per click marketing is at reaching your business objectives. This tracking is different from goal tracking in that goal tracking is all-encompassing. With goals in place, you can track conversion actions no matter what source they originate from.

Google Ads conversion tracking is strictly used to track the effectiveness of your paid search campaigns and, as such, only allows you to track traffic and actions that directly originate from a visitor clicking on one of your paid search ads.

Tracking Google Ads conversions can be done two different ways:.

The first way is tracking progress directly inside the Google Ads interface—this requires a unique tracking code to be placed within the site or application that is independent from the Google Analytics tracking code that may already be present.

The second method of tracking Google Ads campaigns can be done inside Google Analytics. This tracking requires linking your Google Analytics account with your Google Ads account.

I recommend both methods be used in conjunction because doing so provides a system of checks and balances for reporting and provides an additional opportunity for audience remarketing outside of just Google Ads audiences alone.

In addition, tracking conversion data directly inside Google Ads can help with keyword quality scores and CPC bidding, as well as offer additional methods for account optimization that can't be gained by tracking Google Ads conversion inside Google Analytics.

How to Set Up Google Ads Conversion Tracking

So it's now clear there are two ways to track Google Ads conversion data. The first method focuses on tracking conversion data directly inside Google Ads.

In order to set up Google Ads conversion tracking, you must first have a Google Ads account. The tracking snippet you insert on your page(s) for conversion tracking is different from that which you use to track standard "Vanilla" Google Analytics.

The steps to set up conversion tracking in Google Ads are as follows:

1. Log in to your Google Ads account.

2. Click the icon that looks like a wrench (or on the **Tools** menu item in the old style conversion interface) and choose **Conversions**.

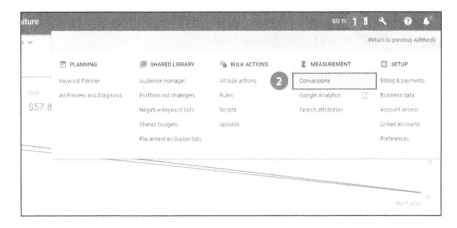

3. On the page that follows, click the **+** button to add a new conversion.

4. Choose what type of conversion you want to set up.

For most ecommerce stores you should select **Website** (and maybe **Phone calls** from ads for brick and mortar stores.)

Give your action a name and complete each of the form elements before saving it. An explanation of each of the elements follows:

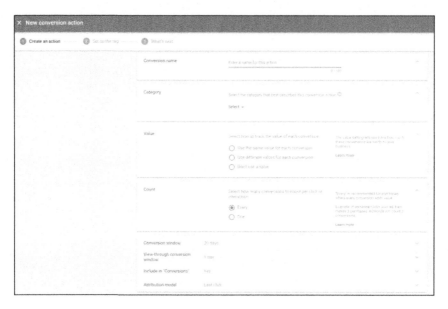

Conversion name: This is the name of the action. Make it something identifiable with what the action represents. For an ecommerce site tracking online sales, this might be Website Sale.

Category: Choose the category this action represents. For ecommerce sites tracking sales, this might be Purchase/Sale. However if you are tracking form opt-ins where a user provides you with an email address in exchange for a report download, for example, then you might want to select **Lead** as the option.

Whatever you choose, make sure the action fits the conversion being tracked.

Value: Choose a value for your conversion. For ecommerce stores tracking sales this choice would most often be **Use different values for each conversion.** When this amount is chosen, the tracking code provided once complete would need to be updated according to your shopping cart specs to dynamically fill in the order value.

If each of your conversions has the exact same value, then choose **Use the same value for each conversion.** If your conversion doesn't translate to a value (maybe in the case of a free download as an example) then choose **Don't use a value.**

Count: Conversions can be recorded in various ways. If one click can lead to many conversions (as is the case with most ecommerce sites) then choose **Every** here because each additional sale from the single click adds value to the business. Choose **One** if you feel each sale does not directly add additional business value (as might be the case with a free download).

Conversion window: This is the amount of time that you are willing to assign a single conversion to a single click. If your customers click your ads and don't typically purchase immediately, use a higher value here. If you don't know then leave this set to the default.

View-through conversions: View through conversions occur when a search triggers your ad (i.e. an impression) but the customer doesn't click the ad and then later ends up converting on your site anyhow. Example: A potential customer searches for "rustic furniture" on the internet, and your ad is triggered but they do not click it. A week later, she hears an ad for your store on the radio and decides to visit it by typing the URL directly into her browser. She completes a purchase and the action is recorded under "view through conversions."

Include in "conversions": In most cases you'll leave this set to **Yes** so the conversions appear in the proper columns within your Google Ads interface. If set to **No,** even if an ad triggers a conversion, it will not be counted.

Attribution model: This lets you set when a conversion will be recorded for this action. Be careful what you choose here as it will affect the way conversions are reported. Use what's best for your business objectives. As an example, if **Last Click** is chosen, then all conversions will be counted based on the last click the user completed before converting on your site. Anything else before that will be ignored. Choosing **First Click** yields the exact opposite results.

After you have all of your variables in place click **Save**. Once you save, you'll see a page like the following:

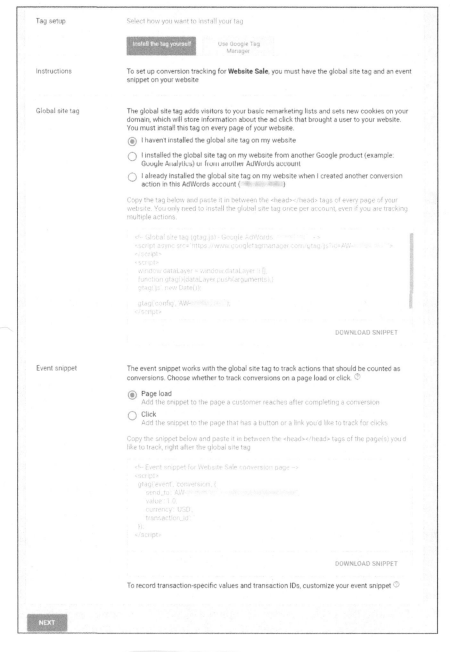

Note: If you want dynamic revenue figures to replace the static version (for example on the order "thank you" page after a sale) then have your technical team replace the number just after the *value=* part of the tracking code. In this example, the "1.0" would be replaced by the dynamic variable which would pull the actual order total and insert it into that same location based upon the unique specifications of the shopping system being used.

Follow the instructions on the screen for copying and inserting the code onto your website. As an optional step you may have Google go out and verify the code is present and installed correctly on your site. This is not always possible however, especially in cases where the page the code resides on requires other actions to occur first (like a customer placing an order with your site).

In these types of instances, Google will not be able to verify the code so the best method of verification is to complete a test order yourself and then view the source on the "thank you" page (from within your browser). To verify the code, look for the presence of the conversion tracking code and/or watch your Google Analytics/Google Ads reporting for the conversion to appear.

Note: If you are going to perform the verification yourself, you must first click on one of your Google Ads ads to access your site or else the conversion tracking will not trigger. This is because the tracking code you are inserting is only used to track the effectiveness of your Google Ads campaigns. For it to work, a visitor must arrive at your site by clicking one of your search ads first. If visitors arrive by any other means, the conversion (for Google Ads purposes) will not be recorded.

You are now set up and ready to track conversion of your paid search campaigns inside the Google Ads interface.

The second method of tracking Google Ads conversion data is inside Google Analytics. To track in this way, you need to link your Google Ads account with your Google Analytics account.

Linking Google Ads to Google Analytics

For even more powerful reporting capabilities, it's a good idea to link your Google Ads and Google Analytics accounts together. This combination provides exceptional reporting capabilities and advertising options, helping you make better decisions that can impact your conversion.

The first task when linking the two accounts is to make sure you're using the same email address for both your Analytics and Google Ads accounts. In addition, make sure that the Google Ads login email address has admin access for the Analytics account. (Refer to the section titled Giving Access to Outside Users - User Management earlier in this book for instructions on how to do this.)

Now that you have confirmed that the email addresses for both accounts are the same and you have given the Google Ads email address admin access privileges, you can link the two accounts using the following steps:

1. Sign in to your Google Ads account.

2. Choose the wrench icon (or the gear icon if using the old interface) then select **Linked Accounts**. On the page screen that follows select the **Google Analytics** option.

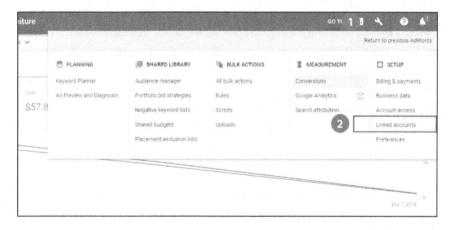

3. Find the property you want to set up a link to and click the **Set Up Link** button. On the screen that follows, choose whether or not you want to import any site metrics. Importing site metrics is an optional step, however, doing so will provide you with a wealth of information not readily available inside Google Ads alone. If you want more insight, I recommend importing the data.

4. Click **Save.**

On newer versions of Google Ads you have the option to also enable Google Optimize account linking from this screen. Google Optimize is a tool used to conduct on-site testing of page elements in an effort to increase conversion.

Google Optimize is often combined with specialized Google Ads campaigns that drive traffic to targeted landing pages and then test various messages and graphical elements to find out which combinations produce higher conversion rates.

Even if you are not utilizing this excellent tool at the moment, it is recommended you turn this feature on so it's ready to share data when that time comes.

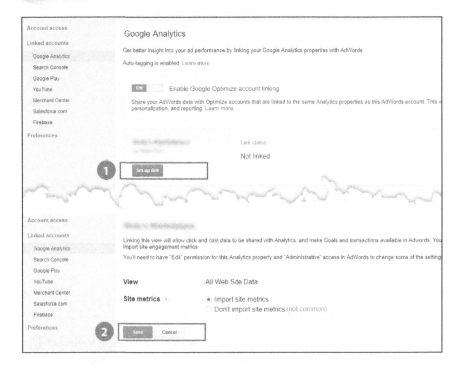

Your Google Ads and Google Analytics accounts should now be linked. If you opted to keep auto-tagging turned on when you set up the website profile for the site you are tracking, then Analytics will start automatically tagging your Google Ads links with information that can be used to get better reporting within Google Analytics.

If you didn't set up auto-tagging it's quick and easy. Follow these steps to turn auto-tagging on:

If using the new Google Ads interface, log in to your Google Ads account and follow these steps:

1. Click **All Campaigns** from the left side.

2. Click **Settings**.

3. Click the **Account Settings** tab.

4.   Click **Edit** and checkmark the box to turn auto-tagging on.

If using the old Google Ads interface, log in to your Google Ads account and follow these steps:

1.   Click the gear icon.

2.   Choose **Account Settings.**

3.   Click **Edit** next to the tracking option and turn that on.

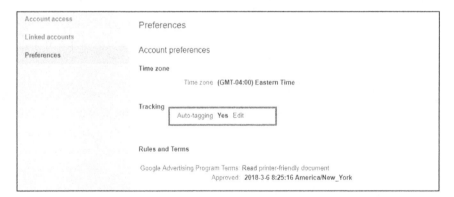

What Type of Information Do Reports Include?

With Google Ads conversion tracking, you'll gain valuable insights on how effectively your digital marketing campaigns are meeting your company objectives. More specifically, you can expect to get detailed reports on keyword conversion rates (how well individual keywords are converting to sales), ad conversion rates (how well your ads are converting visitors to sales), cost per sale/conversion (the amount of money it costs you to make a sale), the overall conversion rate of each campaign you are running, and more.

What You Can Learn From the Tracking Results

The report data you receive when using Google Ads conversion tracking provides a wealth of information and insight into the effectiveness of your paid search campaigns.

Conversion tracking is a methodical process that involves time to perfect. The elements involved can be complex. Understanding them is the key to running a successful campaign that increases your conversion, and makes the most of your money spent.

For starters, if you do not have a lot of traffic coming to your website, Google Ads can get you traffic fast. Conversion tracking can help you determine what your potential customers are looking for, what causes them to buy your product, and what really should be considered qualified traffic for your site. The results may surprise you.

These important elements will provide excellent insight into your visitors' demographic behavior and buying habits—invaluable information if you plan on increasing conversion.

In short, if you don't know what your customers really want, use conversion tracking to help you find out. Once you know what they are looking for and what causes them to buy, you've taken a positive step toward increasing the performance of your marketing efforts, your website, and subsequently, your sales.

Take a look at a few actual statistics you will receive using conversion tracking and see how they can help you increase conversion.

Keyword Conversion: Understanding which keywords actually convert to sales is extremely important. Too often I hear people saying "paid search costs too much to make it worthwhile for me. It costs me more money to get traffic than I make from selling my product."

This couldn't be further from the truth. Paid search, when run and tracked properly, can be a valuable way to increase sales and learn more about your ideal customer base. It starts by understanding your keyword conversion.

Pay careful attention to the conversion rate of individual keywords. It's not wise to bid on keywords that do not convert to sales. Remember, all traffic is not created equal. Driving mass amounts of traffic in the hopes of increasing sales is not the answer. Doing so, in the end, will only cost you money.

However, driving *qualified* traffic (i.e. traffic that has a desire to buy your product) will make you money, and cost you less. Determining which traffic is qualified, and which is not, well, that is where your keyword conversion statistic comes in.

It works like this: If a keyword's conversion rate is positive, and the cost per conversion for that keyword is lower than the revenue you receive from an average sale, then it would be smart to keep that keyword active in your campaign because it is making you money.

On the other hand, if a keyword's conversion rate is low, and if the cost to get traffic from that keyword (cost per conversion) is higher than an average sale from your store, then you should either stop bidding on that keyword, or test new ad copy and other variations of the page you are sending traffic to in an attempt to find out what might increase conversion.

Successful campaigns start by understanding that it's the combination of keyword conversion, cost per conversion, and ad conversion that will ultimately make you money.

Below is a simple illustration that represents how keyword conversion can either make you money or cost you money ... even if you are generating sales from those keywords. It also reinforces the concept that all traffic is not created equal.

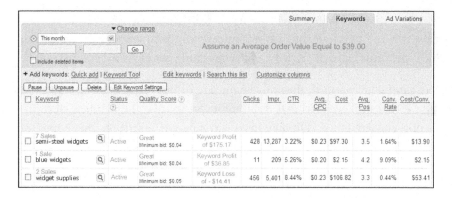

In the illustration above, two keywords are making you money while one keyword is costing you money ... even though all three have generated sales for your store.

Keyword 1, "semi-steel widgets," generated 7 sales over the period analyzed. It drove 428 visitors to the website, and converted 1.64 percent of those visitors to sales at a cost per sale (conversion) of only $13.90. Assuming an average order value of $39.00, you make a profit of $25.10 per sale, for every sale at your store.

Keyword 2, "blue widgets," generated 1 sale over the period analyzed. It drove 11 visitors to the website and converted 9.09 percent of them to sales at a cost per sale (conversion) of just $2.15. Assuming an average order value of $39.00, you make a profit of $36.85 per sale, for every sale at your store.

Keyword 3, "widget supplies," generated 2 sales over the period analyzed. This keyword drove the most traffic (visitors) to the website (456 total) and converted .44 percent of those visitors to sales at a cost per sale (conversion) of $53.41. Assuming an average order value of $39.00, you actually lose $14.41 on every sale you generate from your store. That's not a good sign, and is just like giving your product away for free!

Keyword 3 is also a good example of all traffic not being created equal. Keyword 3 drove the highest amount of traffic to your website, yet resulted in a net loss. This proves the point that driving more traffic to a website in the hopes of making more money is an incorrect methodology that will only hurt you in the end.

Given this example above, it would be wise to continue bidding on the keywords "semi-steel widgets" and "blue widgets." However, you should stop bidding on the keyword "widget supplies" altogether or test different landing pages or ad copy because you lose money with every sale you make by way of that keyword.

Cost per Conversion: As briefly mentioned above; If your cost per conversion is lower than your average sales value (the average total amount of a single order from your store), then you are making money (not taking into consideration LTV factors.) If not, you need to re-think your bids, prices, keywords, ad copy, or all of these factors. Testing is the key here.

Ad Conversion Rate: Like the keyword conversion rate, your ad conversion rate will tell you which ads are generating positive sales and conversion. You should react to your ad conversion rate by split-testing different variations of ad copy in order to find out what prompts the visitors who click those ads to buy.

Furthermore, split-testing copy allows you to play with different variations of terminology to attract more qualified traffic to your site, thereby reducing costs and increasing sales.

Examples of how you could attract more qualified traffic with different ad copy follows. These examples were taken from a real world Google Ads campaign designed to push traffic toward an ecommerce website. (The URLs have been changed for privacy.) These examples are for illustrative purposes only, and the terminology used does not mean it will work for your business. Keep in mind that markets and customers vary.

Example 1:	Example 2:
The following ad attracted more traffic, but that traffic was less qualified. As a result, the cost to attract the traffic was higher, and the sales conversion was lower.	*This ad attracted less traffic to the site, but that traffic was more qualified to buy the product. As a result, both conversion and sales increased.*
Get Child Growth Charts	Shop Child Growth Charts
Unique Wall Hanging Measuring	Free Shipping, Wall Hung

Charts to Track Your Child's Growth	Measuring Charts to track your child's growth
www.yourdomain.com	www.yourdomain.com
Average Sales Value = $39.00 Ad Conversion Rate = .24 percent Cost per Conversion = $39.35	Average Sales Value = $39.00 Ad Conversion Rate = 1.5 percent Cost per Conversion = $15.74
This ad cost the company money, and produced a "net loss." (It cost $39.35 to get a sale of $39.00: a loss of $.35 with every sale.)	*By simply altering the terminology in the ad, this ad made the company money. It cost less and attracted more qualified traffic.* **Increased Conversion over 600 percent** **Net profit increase of 247 percent**

Keep in mind that although the above illustration was taken from a real-world example, the individual results may vary from market to market, and ad split-testing should be utilized to determine what works for your market segment.

HELPFUL HINT

Google Ads conversion tracking is used to analyze the effectiveness of your paid search (Google Ads) campaigns. Conversion tracking begins when a user clicks on one of your ads, and ideally ends when they take an action on your site (such as buy your product).

Thus, conversion tracking will record *only* those visitors and actions which originate directly from one of your paid search ads. It will *not* record visitors and actions that come from sources other than paid search.

7

TRACKING ON-SITE SEARCH

If you offer on-site search functionality, it's important to know what visitors are searching for while at your site. Google Analytics offers the ability to track this through the Site Search feature.

What Is Site Search?

When you activate Site Search tracking within Google Analytics you enable tracking of the on-site search form on your website. Site Search provides you with a way to deliver reporting metrics about how users interact with the search functionality on your site: what types of search queries they perform, what happens after the search takes place, and more. Without tracking Site Search, these metrics would otherwise be hidden from view.

What Can Site Search Do for Your Business?

Understanding how users interact with your website search form is critical in delivering more relevant information, which in turn leads to increased conversion and often sales. Without tracking on-site searches, you have no idea what occurs from the moment a visitor decides to search to the moment he either makes a purchase or leaves your website.

Knowing more about this process can make all the difference in building a more user-friendly experience and might even lead to additional product development ideas you may not have considered before.

Consider this real-world example from a website that implemented Site Search tracking:

An ecommerce retailer offered a single product in 12 different printable standard-style variations. Sales were okay, but something was missing. The retailer's site had very targeted traffic yet a decent portion of visitors left and did not buy. After activating tracking for on-site search functionality, it soon became clear what was occurring.

Although the visitors arriving to the site were typically qualified to buy the product, the style offered was not what they were looking for. By analyzing the reports detailing what occurred with the search form on the site it was determined that many of the visitors performed searches on a style of product that the store did not offer. The store offered 12 standard variations, but the visitors wanted a more customized version of the exact same product.

After learning this from report analysis, the store decided to offer a new variation of the same product. The new variation started blank and allowed customers to customize the final look based upon their own needs by uploading images. Giving visitors the ability to make the product appear exactly as they wanted it to resulted in increased sales across the board.

The information learned from Site Search was a valuable tool that directly increased sales for this store. What the owners learned prompted them to add a new style to their existing product line and it proved to be a game changer. Prior to implementing Site Search there simply was no easy way to discover that a majority of visitors wanted a more custom product. After tracking on-site search it was evident.

How Do You Set Up Site Search?

1. Log in to Google Analytics and go to **Admin** > **View Settings** for the property you want to set up Site Search tracking on.

2. Turn **Site search Tracking** on, then enter the query parameters. Details on how to find your query parameters are listed below the image.

3. Enter the **Query parameter** that represents your search string in the URL.

4. To find the parameter that designates the search query keywords on your site, do the following:

   a. Navigate to your site through a browser and perform an actual search using the form on your site. Take note of the term(s) you use to perform the search. They don't need to return any results at this time; you are simply using these terms to identify the query parameter that represents them. In the example below the terms "test search" were entered.

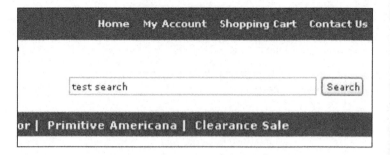

b. After performing the search, look at the address bar of the browser to find the portion of the URL that includes the keywords you entered. In the example, "test search" was entered as appears in URL below.

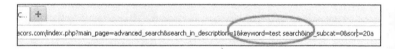

c. After you find the keywords you searched on in the URL, look to the portion just left of that (just before the equal sign) to find your search query parameter. In this example the parameter is highlighted below and is represented by the parameter named "keyword."

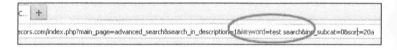

d. Now take that term and insert it into the box provided under the **Query paramater** field (refer to the image on the prior page for an example.)

    You may optionally select to strip out any additional query parameters from the URL if desired. Stripping out any added parameters removes these from your reports, which could help clean out some unnecessary items.

    In this example the following parameters, which mean nothing for reporting purposes, could be stripped: *search_in_description, sort.*

e. If you want to track search based on categories you would follow the steps b, c, and d above except that you would be looking for any parameter that indicates a category ID.

(Hint: when you perform the search, perform it from within a category page.)

f. In the example in section b above, the parameter that designates a category is indicated by the *sub_cat* portion of the URL.

8

DEMOGRAPHICS AND INTEREST BASED REPORTING

What Is Demographics and Interest Based Reporting?

Demographic and interest data report on users' age and gender, along with interests they show while navigating online or completing purchase activities.

What Can This Reporting Do for My Business?

Understanding the demographics and interests of your visitors can help you refine further advertising efforts and even help guide improvements for design. From an advertising perspective, this kind of reporting can provide information on where to advertise and what audiences to target, whether it be for conversion or branding. Example: If your visitors show an interest in travel, you may want to consider placing advertising on sites specific to travel.

On the other hand, if you sell a product targeting senior men, and your demographic data indicates most of your traffic comes from men ages 18-35, then you need to reconsider your message and advertising.

How to Activate Interest Based Reporting

You have two options for enabling the Demographics and Interest Reports in Google Analytics.

Enabling from the Admin tab:

1. Log in to your Google Analytics account.

2. Click on the gear icon to get to the **Admin** tab.

3. Choose the **Property** you want to activate demographic reporting for and then turn on the switch by **Enable Demographics and Interest Reports** section.

Enabling from the Reports section:

1. Log in to your Google Analytics account.

2. Navigate to the **Account, Property,** and **View** that you want to activate the reporting for.

3. From the report options choose **Audience > Demographics >**

Overview. If reporting hasn't yet been activated you can turn it on using the switch on this page. It would look similar to the following:

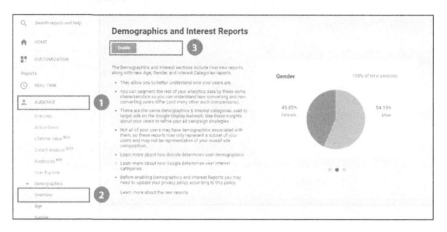

What Type of Reports Can I Expect?

Currently, seven standard reports are available:

Demographics Overview: The overview report shows data breakdowns on gender and age. It typically defaults to views on the users' key metric, but can be changed to view data on any of the following: sessions, pages per session, bounce rate, average session duration, and percent of new sessions.

Age: Data in this report is broken down by age group. You can further drill down to gender by clicking an age group range.

Gender: Data in this report is first broken down by gender. Further drilling down shows breakdowns by age group and then by interest within that gender.

Interests Overview: This report shows the top 10 interests across in-market segments, affinity categories, and other categories.

Affinity Categories (reach): Metrics in this report are broken down by affinity categories. With affinity audience targeting, rather than looking at a visitor's purchase intent (as is the case with in-market reporting) the focus is on overall interests and lifestyle.

In-Market Segments: Metrics in this report are broken down by in-market segments. Unlike affinity categories, in–market audiences are actively searching for and likely comparing your product or service to others. Visitors who fit into this audience have shown that they are interested in and shopping for items within a certain category such as "home and garden," "apparel & accessories," or "travel."

Other Categories: Metrics in this report are broken down by other categories.

What You Can Learn From the Tracking Results

As mentioned earlier, activating Demographics and Interest Reports can help you better focus your advertising efforts. Finding out which demographics are more inclined to purchase your product or service can lead to more targeted ad placements.

For example: If you find out that women ages 25-34 convert at a higher rate than other people, you might want to increase your bidding on ads targeting that range. Likewise, if you find that a majority of your high-converting visitors are interested in sports and fitness, it may be advantageous to consider testing ads on specific sites that cover topics like sports nutrition, exercise, and so on. On the other hand, demographic reporting can also indicate possible reasons why your product isn't selling as expected. Example: An auto dealer selling high-end luxury automobiles with base prices starting at $300,000 is targeting middle-age executives. The dealership's site receives plenty of traffic but sales are lagging.

The owner digs into the demographic reporting and finds the majority of visitors are in the 18-24 age group. Although more analysis is needed, upon first glance he could surmise that the young visitors do not have high enough income levels to support buying one of these cars but are searching for luxury cars out of interest only. They may have heard about the brand and are curious what the cars look like.

Armed with this data, further analysis can be conducted and if needed, adjustments made to the dealer's advertising efforts to weed out age groups that don't fit the target.

9

REMARKETING

What Is Remarketing?

Most often, remarketing means advertising to people who have visited your site or used your mobile app and left without completing an action (making a purchase for an ecommerce store). Although this is the most common method of remarketing, you can also remarket to visitors who have completed an action on your site, such as those who added an item to their cart or completed the checkout.

Remarketing is also referred to as retargeting, although some people make a distinction between the two terms from a technical perspective. Purists use remarketing to describe advertising to those who have completed an action on the site (i.e. are a current customer) and prefer the term retargeting when marketing to those who have not completed an action. Google uses the term remarketing regardless of who the target is and for purposes of this guide, I'll keep it that way.

Remarketing as a whole is actually served through an advertiser (in this case Google Ads), however, it's being covered here because getting the maximum benefit from it involves combining Google Analytics and Google Ads. For that reason, this topic crosses over both Google Ads and

Analytics in an effort to provide insight on combining the two forces and why you would want to.

What Can Remarketing Do for My Business?

Any business using Google Ads for marketing should consider running at least one remarketing campaign. Remarketing provides a wealth of opportunity for re-engaging visitors and increasing sales.

Use it to target visitors who arrive at your site and don't complete an action, as well as targeting visitors who have completed an action. Here are some ideas on how to use remarketing as part of your advertising strategy:

Abandoned cart recovery: Most ecommerce sites have a system in place to recover abandoned carts. However, these systems are often only effective if customers begin the checkout process and provide information about themselves, including and most important, their email address. In the event of abandonment, the email address is used to send a series of follow-ups to customers in an attempt to get them to complete the checkout.

What happens though when customers add an item to their shopping cart, don't begin the checkout process, and then leave? How can you contact them? Using remarketing we can set up a few lists to accomplish this: One list for those who added an item to their cart, one for those who completed the checkout, and a combination list of both so we can target those that are in the add to cart list but not in the checkout complete list. Instructions on how to set each of the three lists up is detailed later on in this chapter.

HELPFUL HINT

It should be noted that Google Ads has the option to automatically create some default remarketing lists, and for retail sites, one of them represents abandoned carts. However, to make this work properly, the tracking code across the site needs to be updated by adding the *ecomm_pagetype* variable along with data for which page it represents on the site. Example: *ecomm_pagetype="product"* translates to the product page of the website while *ecomm_pagetype="cart"* translates to the shopping cart page.

This isn't always easy, and depending on the solution being used, might not be an option at all. For that reason, I prefer the method detailed later in this chapter over the alternative.

Re-engage prospects: Prospects are visitors who haven't yet become customers. Remarketing to them is one way to win their business. Dynamic remarketing is a great option for retailers to re-engage prospects because it shows the most relevant ads to them based on their interests.

Combined with a product feed, dynamic remarketing has the ability to show customized ads tailored to specific products the visitor showed interest in while navigating the site or app.

Re-engage current customers: Keeping in front of current customers using remarketing is a great way to stay at the top of their mind when branding.

A more creative use of remarketing can be achieved when developed in conjunction with individual customer buying habits. Take the case of a client I worked with who sold expendable products, in this case coffee.

After first analyzing the data on average time it took customers to go through their coffee and then reorder, I set up a remarketing campaign for those buyers based on average reorder time from the point of last purchase.

Knowing the average time it took for customers to reorder, the campaign was set up to begin showing ads to them a week or so before they would typically need to reorder. The creative of the ads revolved around messaging reminding customers it was time to reorder, thus keeping the client at the top of their mind at a point when they would typically begin searching to replenish their coffee inventory.

Dynamic vs. Static Remarketing

Remarketing comes in two flavors: dynamic and static. Which method you choose will depend on your business type and objectives.

Dynamic remarketing targets visitors based on *specific* interests they showed while using a website or app. A unique ad is created for each individual visitor based upon those interests. Dynamic ads use machine learning technology to analyze visitor behavior and determine what creative elements might persuade the visitor to return to the site to complete a purchase.

Dynamic remarketing works well for ecommerce stores that have big product catalogs because it saves both time and money while being able to serve visitors who left the site ads containing specific products they viewed while there.

Here is an example of how remarketing works: A visitor arrives at a website that sells sporting goods. The visitor looks at a catcher's mitt and then leaves. While the visitor continues to navigate the internet, the remarketing partner gathers data on his behavior across all devices. It then uses machine learning to develop an algorithm that places a personalized ad with the catcher's mitt in front of the visitor when he is most likely to convert.

Static remarketing targets visitors based on pages they visit on your site. The ads aren't as customized as those with dynamic remarketing, but can include persuasive content related to an overall category (in the case of ecommerce retailers). Static remarketing is a good option for those trying to build brand awareness or increase leads.

Here is an example of how static remarketing might work: A campaign is created around an online educational course. Several ads are developed and each is triggered based on different pages a visitor browses. One ad may target those who actually viewed the course while another targets visitors who read content relating to the course but who didn't actually land on the course page.

Dynamic remarketing should be considered if:

- You're an ecommerce business selling products that appeal to a wide range of customers.

- You sell more than one product type, have a large inventory, and have multiple product categories.

- Your customer base is broad and the intentions vary widely when customers visit your site.

- Your customers each have unique tastes, wants, and needs in relation to the products offered. An example might be two customers who both like fishing rods but one of them prefers fly rods while the other prefers deep sea rods.

Static remarketing should be considered if:

- The purpose of your business is to generate leads.

- You are interested in branding and awareness.

- You are an online retailer with a small product line.

- You want to remarket to visitors but are only promoting a single offer.

- You want ads that target different broad types of customers but not individual customers.

- You want more control over the ad creative. Whereas dynamic remarketing auto creates the ads for you, static remarketing is more hands-on, enabling you to craft a very specific look, feel, and message.

When setting up a dynamic remarketing campaign, there are a few items you need to have in place before you start or the campaign won't work.

1. Ensure you have a Google Merchant Center account and that you are sending data to it regularly via a product feed.

2. Make sure your data feed is up to date and optimized for SEO.

3. Your Merchant Center account and Google Ads accounts must be linked. (Linking the two is covered in this chapter.)

Enable Remarketing and Advertising Reporting Features in Google Analytics

Setting up remarketing to gain maximum benefit is a multi-step process that involves enabling remarketing and reporting capability for the Analytics property (this is typically done within Google Analytics), tagging your site with remarketing code (from Google Ads), creating audiences and lists (in both Analytics and Google Ads), and finally, for maximum benefit, linking your Google Analytics account to your Google Ads account.

If you plan on doing any online advertising, it's wise to enable remarketing and advertising reporting features. Doing so allows you to create extremely refined remarketing audiences in Analytics based on user interaction with your site or app and share those audiences with advertising accounts like Google Ads.

Wait, can't you create audiences in Google Ads? Yes you can, however, by creating audiences using Google Analytics you introduce a whole new level of detail for remarketing that Google Ads alone can't provide. Best of all, you can use both Analytics and Google Ads at the same time to create audience targets for remarketing and in fact, doing so provides the widest options for remarketing.

You can enable remarketing and advertising reporting features for a web property by using one of the following methods:

- Modifying your property settings from within Google Analytics. This is the preferred and easiest method.

- Modifying your Google Analytics tracking code.

Enabling remarketing and advertising reporting features from within Google Analytics is the easiest and preferred method. It requires no code updates, and allows you to create more refined audiences that can be shared with your Google Ads account when linked.

In addition, enabling remarketing settings using this method is also the only way you will be able to use the Analytics tag to create Remarketing Lists for Search Ads (RLSA) within Google Analytics.

To update your property settings, follow these steps:

- Log in to your Google Analytics account, click the **Admin** link, and navigate to the property you want these features enabled for.

- Choose **Tracking Info > Data Collection** under the property you want to enable remarketing data collection for.

- Turn both the **Remarketing** *and* **Advertising Reporting Features** selections **On.**

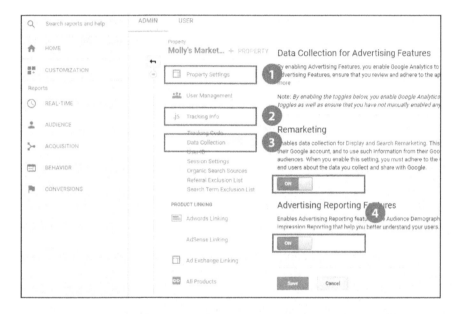

If you already updated your tracking code at an earlier date to enable the remarketing and advertising reporting features there should be no conflicts by also changing the property settings and you can safely leave everything as is.

You can also enable remarketing and advertising reporting features by modifying your tracking code, however, the preferred method of enabling them is to modify your property settings as described above.

Also remember, if you ever want to use Remarketing Lists for Search Ads (RLSA), you must enable remarketing using the property settings method listed in the prior section—you will not be able to run those if you modify the tracking code only.

To modify your tracking code you need to just add the following line to your current code snippet:

```
ga('require', 'displayfeatures');
```

An example of what the full tracking code might look like once inserted is as follows:

```
<script>
(function(i,s,o,g,r,a,m){i['GoogleAnalyticsObject']=r;i[r]=
i[r]||function(){
(i[r].q=i[r].q||[]).push(arguments)},i[r].l=1*new
Date();a=s.createElement(o),
m=s.getElementsByTagName(o)[0];a.async=1;a.src=g;m.parentNo
de.insertBefore(a,m)
})(window,document,'script','//www.google-
analytics.com/analytics.js','ga');
ga('create', 'UA-XXXXXX-XX', 'example.com');
ga('require', 'displayfeatures');
ga('send', 'pageview');
</script>
```

Setting Up Remarketing and Tagging Your Site

Enabling remarketing and advertising reporting features in Google Analytics gives you the ability to create targeted audiences. However, to be able to show ads to those audiences you need to tag your site with a tracking code snippet.

Note: Any advertiser that uses the *new* Google Ads interface to set up remarketing will notice there is now one global tracking code snippet and an optional event tracking snippet. If you have the previous Google Ads remarketing tag installed on your site, it will still work with no conflicts, however, Google recommends switching to the new tag.

Tagging your site using the old Google Ads interface

To set up remarketing inside Google Ads using the old interface:

- Log in to your Google Ads account, click the **Campaigns** tab, and choose **Shared library > Audiences > Set up remarketing.**

The page that follows will look something like this:

For standard remarketing leave the checkbox blank. For dynamic ads checkmark the box that fits your industry—online retailers select **Retail** from the drop-down list. After making your choices, click **Set up remarketing.**

IMPORTANT NOTE

Keep in mind that to use dynamic remarketing you'll need to submit a product feed to Google. If you do not submit a feed your ads will not work. You do not need a feed if you leave the checkbox blank and plan on using conventional/static remarketing.

On the page that follows click on **View Google Ads tag for websites**.

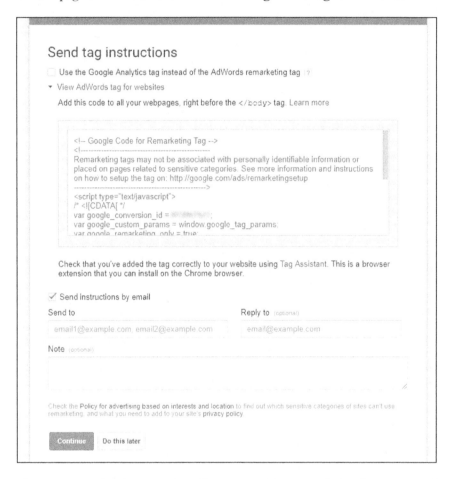

If you use a developer to install your tracking, you have the option of emailing him or her with the instructions from here. If however you manage your own site and are able to add the tracking code yourself, copy the tracking code from the window provided and follow the on-screen instructions to paste it into your site and publish it.

When you create your first remarketing campaign, a new list will automatically be created for you to start with called All Visitors.

Your tag should start collecting data from visitors to your website within a couple of days and your All Visitors list will begin to populate.

You can verify the tag is in place by navigating to **Shared Library > Audiences**. It may take up to 24 hours to validate the tag. If your tag is not working you need to:

1. Visit your site and view the source from within a browser to ensure the tracking code is in place.

2. Make sure the tracking code is on every page of the site and in the proper position.

If everything is working you should see a message similar to the following:

If your list doesn't begin to populate in several days, go back and ensure all the steps were completed properly and try to validate it again.

Tagging your site using the new Google Ads interface

To set up remarketing inside Google Ads using the new interface:

- Log in to Google Ads and choose the tool icon.

- Next select **Audience Manager** under the **Shared Library** section.

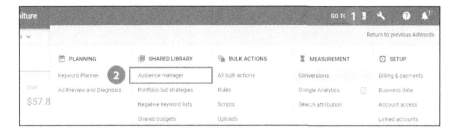

- On the left, click **Audience** sources.

- In the **Google Ads tag** card, click **Set Up Tag**.

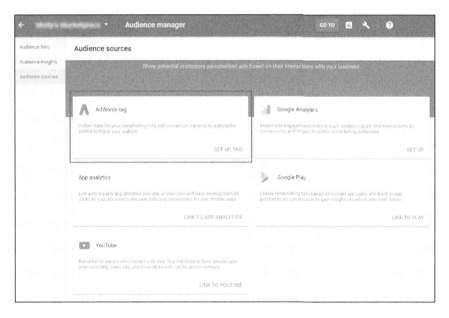

Note: If you have already set up a tag, click the 3-dot icon in the upper right section of the **Google Ads tag** card and choose **Edit** source.

- Choose which type of data the tag will collect. **Standard data** is the same as static remarketing and **Specific attributes/parameters** is the equivalent of dynamic remarketing.

  When you choose standard data you also have the option of choosing to include the user ID parameter with the tag. Adding this enables you to show even more targeted ads to individual (unique) visitors.

When you choose specific attributes or parameters you also choose the business type that represents your products or services. For ecommerce stores this would be **Retail.**

- Click **Create and Continue** (or **Save and Continue** for an existing tag).

Next you'll be presented with the installation screen where you will get the tracking code snippet. It looks similar to this:

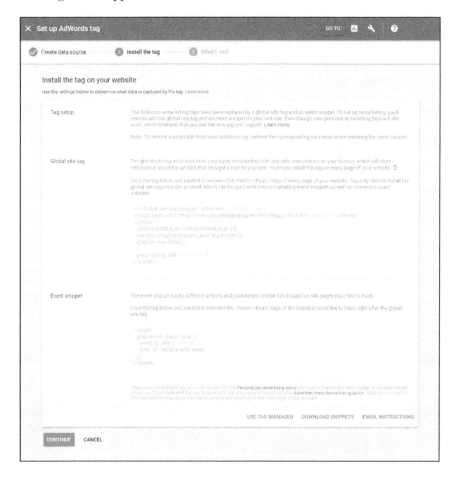

Copy the code and install it into your site according to the instructions (or set up using Tag Manager if that is your preferred method), download the code snippets for later use, or email the instructions to your web developer to complete.

While the global site tag needs to be added to every page on your site regardless of the type of campaign you are running, for dynamic remarketing campaigns, the event snippet only needs to be placed on the specific pages you want to track for dynamic remarketing events.

HELPFUL HINT

If you have already added the global site tag to your site via another means (as would be the case if using the Google Analytics global site tag or from a prior conversion tracking event you added) then you do not need to add it again. You still need to add the event snippet on the pages you might want to target for dynamic events.

Optional: If you previously added the global site tag using Google Analytics, you can add the 'config' command from the Google Ads tag (shown in bold below) to every single instance of the tag. An example of what it might look like is below (where 123456789 is replaced with your actual customer ID).

```
<script async
src="https://www.googletagmanager.com/gtag/js?id=AW-
123456789"></script>
<script>
window.dataLayer = window.dataLayer || [];
function gtag(){dataLayer.push(arguments);}
gtag('js', new Date());

gtag('config', 'AW-123456789');

</script>
```

As another option, if you're using an event snippet for remarketing and don't want the global site tag to send an extra hit, modify the tracking by placing the line shown below, under the config line in the tracking snippet (where 123456789 is replaced with your own tracking ID).

```
gtag('config', 'AW-123456789', {'send_page_view': false});
```

- Once complete, click **Continue.**

Validate the new code is in place correctly using either one of Google's tag validation tools, or by waiting a few days and checking the **Google Ads tag** card.

Validation in the new interface might look like this:

Remarketing Audiences and Lists

After tagging your site with the tracking code, it's time to define some remarketing lists and audiences. Note: When you set up remarketing for the first time, a few standard lists/audiences were automatically created for you.

A remarketing list is a subset of site visitors segmented by their on-site activities. Example: One subset might be represented by visitors you want to target based on how far they made it through the checkout while another subset might be represented by visitors who reached a particular product page or category.

A remarketing audience is a list of cookies or mobile-advertising IDs that represents a group of users you want to re-engage because of their likelihood to convert. These remarketing audiences are created based upon their behavior on your site.

Remarketing lists target remarketing audiences.

You build remarketing lists inside Google Ads from the data collected by the remarketing tag and thus these lists are native to Google Ads. You build remarketing audiences in Google Analytics from the data you gather there and thus those are native to Analytics. You can combine the two in Google Ads as long as the Google Ads account is linked to a Google Analytics account.

Create Your First Remarketing Audience

To create an audience in Analytics:

1. Sign in to Google Analytics.

2. Click **Admin**, and navigate to the **Property** in which you want to create the audience.

3. In the **Property** column, click **Audience Definitions > Audiences**.

4. Choose the **Audience source.** As a default, this data comes from the current reporting view level of the account. Any users filtered from the view you use will also be filtered from the audience.

   To change the view, click **Edit**, select a new view, then click **Next step.**

5. Choose **Next Step** to enable remarketing if it asks (or **+New Audience** if you already have set up remarketing). *Note: If choosing* **+New Audience**—*meaning you have already set up remarketing--then you can skip the remainder of these steps and continue to Creating a New Audience.* If you have not set up any audiences previously, then Google Analytics will automatically create your first audience and name it "All Users."

6. Under **Audience destinations,** click **+ Add Destination** and choose all the accounts you wish to share the audience lists with. If you have linked your Google Analytics and Google Ads accounts together already, this is where you'll be able to select that as well.

    If you haven't linked them and want to know how before you complete this step, cancel out of this window and go back to chapter 6 of this guide for details on linking .

After you have selected the destinations to share data with, your screen looks something like this:

7. Click **Enable** to complete the setup.

Creating a New Remarketing Audience

When you set up remarketing in Google Analytics the first time, a default audience named "All Users" is automatically created. But what if you want to create more audiences to target other segments? Follow the same steps as in the previous section, however, at step number 5 your screen will look like the following:

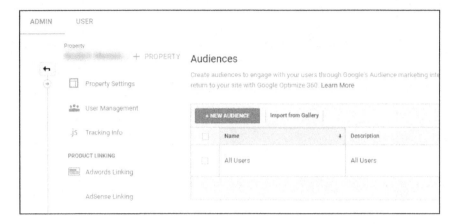

Choose **+New Audience.**

Analytics provides several pre-defined audiences you can use or you can create your own unique audience based on custom criteria.

Choose one of the pre-defined audiences from those provided or create your own then give it a name. This is the name of the audience as it will appear in your reports so make it something descriptive. Then choose **Next Step**. Complete setup from there starting from step 6 in the previous section.

Continue the above process for any other audiences you might want to set up to create your first remarketing campaign.

The pre-defined audiences are listed below along with a short description of what each represents.

Smart List: Choosing this allows Google to manage the audience for you.

All Users: This includes all users of your site or app. It is typically the default audience that is automatically created when you first activate remarketing.

New Users: These represent new visitors only who have completed one session with your site or app.

Returning Users: These are all visitors who have completed more than one session with your site or app.

Users who visited a specific section of my site/app: Click the **Edit** icon, and enter the URL of a page or directory on your site (you can copy and paste the URL if needed), or a screen in your app. Note: The default setting here uses the *contains* match type, so any string (or portion thereof) that you enter here will match any URL which contains it.

Users who completed a goal conversion: If you want to set up an audience based on a specific goal visitors completed at your site (or in your app) use this setting. For example, if you set up a goal for all visitors who added an item to their cart and want to develop an audience around that for remarketing to, choose that goal. Click the **Edit** icon, and select a goal from the menu.

Users who completed a transaction: When choosing this audience, there is no additional configuration needed as it is already configured to include any user with more than zero transactions. Note: For this audience to work, you need to have ecommerce tracking set up.

Custom Remarketing Audiences

Audiences can be pre-defined or custom-created to fit individual needs. One way to set up custom audiences is to import those that fit your business using the **Import from Gallery** tab in the **Audiences** section of Analytics.

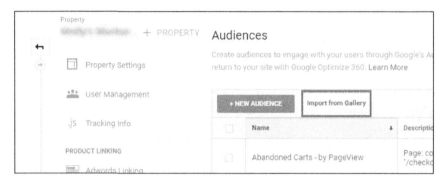

The Google Gallery will lead you to a whole library of custom audiences that have been pre-configured by others and made available for easy import into any Google Analytics setup.

You may not always find what you need there, so here are a few examples to get you started. These custom audiences would be a nice fit for any ecommerce store.

Visitors who dropped out of a funnel

Example funnels:

Category page > Product page > Cart page > Checkout page

The objective would be to re-engage visitors where they dropped out of your conversion funnel.

Do this by creating an audience that includes visitors who completed a particular stage in the funnel and excludes visitors who didn't get to later stages of the funnel.

For example, let's say we want to target visitors who left the site at a specific product page.

We want to include visitors who viewed the category page (e.g., Collections/Dining+Room+Tables) and the product page (e.g., Rustic+Industrial+Wooden+Dining+Room+Table) but exclude visitors who viewed the cart page and the checkout page.

This example includes visitors who showed an interest in the rustic pine dining table, but didn't purchase it. You might consider remarketing to these visitors with ads for that specific dining room table (potentially offering discounts on it) or with ads for similar items.

Users who abandoned items in their shopping carts

Online retailers typically have a remarketing process for visitors who add items to their cart, start the checkout, and provide their email address during that time. Recovery is usually attempted with a follow-up email. But not everyone who adds an item to their cart will begin the checkout process. For these visitors, setting up a remarketing audience in Analytics is the way to reach them.

Build the audience by including visitors who click Add to Cart (or who view the cart page), but exclude visitors who view the order-confirmation page (meaning they completed the checkout process).

There are a number of ways to set this up. Here are examples of two different methods that could be used:

Example 1: Using **Event Action** as the trigger

Example 2: Using the visited **Page** as the trigger

When you use the page as the triggers for both include and exclude filters, you can also opt to remove those that end up purchasing (you recover the abandoned cart) so you don't keep remarketing to them after you win them back. Do this by placing a checkmark in the box next to **Permanently remove users when they match the Exclude condition** on the page that follows after clicking **Apply**.

Users who have never purchased

Looking to gain as many new customers as possible? Then remarketing to visitors who come to your site but have never purchased is a good idea. The types of ads are endless here, but one idea would be to serve them ads with a coupon discount for first time buyers.

To market to those visitors who have come to the site but never purchased you should include the ones whose transactions equal 0, and permanently exclude users when their transactions are greater than 0.

After clicking **Apply** on the previous screen, to permanently remove any visitors who do end up becoming customers checkmark the appropriate box **Permanently remove users when they match the Exclude condition.**

Creating a Remarketing List

Setup of remarketing lists is completed inside Google Ads. Although similar to the audiences in Google Analytics, you don't have as many options for developing lists in Google Ads.

When you set up your first remarketing campaign in Google Ads, Google creates some automatic lists for you. Instructions on how to create additional lists can be found below.

Create a remarketing list in Google Ads using new interface:

- Sign in to Google Ads.

- Click the tool menu icon and then choose **Shared Library > Audience Manager.**

- Click **Audience Lists**.

- Click the **+** button to create a new list and choose your list type. (Website visitors is most common.)

- On the page that opens, give your list/audience a name, choose a template from the **List members** drop-down menu, build a set of rules in the **Visited page** section (click **Add** after building a rule), enter a **Membership duration** (i.e. how long you want members to stay on your list), enter an optional audience **Description,** and click **Create Audience.**

Repeat the above procedure to create additional lists to include in your Google Ads campaigns and ad groups.

HELPFUL HINT

If you created any audiences in Google Analytics and then shared with Google Ads but don't see them listed, check your filter. If a filter is present, either clear it or add Google Analytics as another option by checking the appropriate box.

137

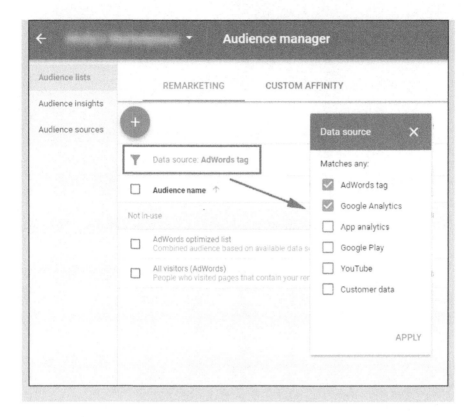

Create a remarketing list in Google Ads using old interface:

- Sign in to Google Ads.

- Click **Campaigns** tab.

- Click **Shared library**.

- Click **Audiences**.

  If you're creating a remarketing list for the first time, you'll see several remarketing options. Under **Website visitors,** click **Set up remarketing** and complete the setup process. This initial setup was covered earlier in the chapter in the section on tagging your site. If this isn't the first remarketing list you've created, click **+Remarketing list** and select **Website visitors** from the drop-down menu.

- On the page that opens, give your list/audience a name, choose a template from the **Who to add to your list** drop-down menu, click **+Rule** to build a set of rules (click **Done** after building a rule), enter a **Membership duration** (i.e. how long you want members to stay on your list), enter an optional audience **Description**, and click **Save**.

Note: If your website already has a remarketing tag on it and you want to include recent visitors who match your list's rules, leave the **Include past visitors that match these rules** box checked. This only works for the Display Network and will not work with remarketing lists for search ads (RLSA).

Repeat the above procedure to create additional lists to include in your Google Ads campaigns and ad groups.

When remarketing, be sure to focus your marketing efforts on how visitors interact with your site. For maximum benefit, the message you convey to them through remarketing should be relevant and fit the point where they are in their buying cycle.

Here are five examples of remarketing lists you might create along with the type of message you could convey to the target.

Image Source: Google

Linking Google Ads to Google Merchant Center

As discussed earlier, in addition to using behavior and intent as a way to serve ads, dynamic remarketing can gather data from a product feed to automatically create ads specific to a user's needs. For this to occur however, your Google Ads account needs to be linked to your Google Merchant Center account so the two can share data.

When you link the two, you also open up the ability to also run Google Shopping ads.

It is worth noting that a request to link Google Ads and Merchant Center can only happen from within the Merchant Center account (i.e. the request has to originate from the Merchant Center account). Any new requests will appear in Google Ads under the **Linked accounts** page under the settings drop-down menu.

It is also worth noting that once the link is made, any ads that are set up that use the data feed as a source for serving ads will stop serving ads if the link is ever removed.

You can link multiple Google Ads accounts to a single Merchant Center account, and a single Google Ads account can be linked to multiple Merchant Center accounts.

To link to your own Google Ads account:

1. In your Merchant Center account, go to the three-dot icon drop-down and then click **Account linking**.

2. Select **Google Ads**.

3. Under **Your Google Ads Account,** find the Google Ads customer ID of the account you want to link. You can find the customer ID at the top of any Google Ads page when you're signed in, near your email address.

4. Click **Link**.

Note: If you don't have an Google Ads account, you can click **Create** **account** *on this page.*

To link to other Google Ads accounts:

1. In your Merchant Center account, go to the three-dot icon drop-down and then click **Account linking**.

2. Select **Google Ads**.

3. Under **Other Google Ads accounts,** enter the Google Ads customer ID of the account you want to link. You can find the customer ID at the top of any Google Ads page when you're signed in, near your email address.

4. Click **Add**.

Once the link is requested, it will need to be approved from within the Google Ads account using the following steps:

1. Click the gear icon, then select **Linked accounts** from **Account settings** and open the **Google Merchant Center** section.

2. Click the **View request** button.

3. Review the request details. Linking the accounts doesn't grant administrative access to either account holder, and either you or the Merchant Center account holder can unlink the accounts at any time.

4. To approve the link, click **Approve**.

   To reject this link, click **Reject** and confirm that you want to reject it. If you want to link these accounts later, you'll need to send a new link request from Merchant Center.

Made in the USA
Monee, IL
12 November 2020